Lecture Notes in Operations Research and Mathematical Systems

Economics, Computer Science, Information and Control

Edited by M. Beckmann, Providence and H. P. Künzi, Zürich

54

C. C. von Weizsäcker

Albert Weber-Institut für Sozial- und Staatswissenschaften
der Universität Heidelberg

Steady State Capital Theory

Springer-Verlag
Berlin · Heidelberg · New York 1971

Advisory Board

H. Albach · A. V. Balakrishnan · F. Ferschl · R. E. Kalman · W. Krelle · N. Wirth

ISBN 3-540-05582-7 Springer-Verlag Berlin Heidelberg New York
ISBN 0-387-05582-7 Springer-Verlag New York Heidelberg Berlin

This work is subject to copyright. All rights are reserved, whether the whole or part of the material is concerned, specifically those of translation, reprinting, re-use of illustrations, broadcasting, reproduction by photocopying machine or similar means, and storage in data banks.

Under § 54 of the German Copyright Law where copies are made for other than private use, a fee is payable to the publisher, the amount of the fee to be determined by agreement with the publisher.

© by Springer-Verlag Berlin · Heidelberg 1971. Library of Congress Catalog Card Number 76-173743. Printed in Germany.

Offsetdruck: Julius Beltz, Hemsbach/Bergstr.

Contents

Preface			1
Part I	Capital Theory without Capital		4
	Chapter 1	The Static Input-Output Model without Substitution	4
	Chapter 2	The Static Input-Output Model with Substitution	8
	Chapter 3	The Static Input-Output Model with more than One Nonproducible Factor of Production	11
Part II	Circulating Capital		15
	Chapter 1	A One Sector Model	15
	Chapter 2	Many Goods, no Substitution	18
	Chapter 3	Dated Labour Inputs and the Theory of Value and Exploitation	22
	Chapter 4	Dated Labour Inputs and the Period of Production	32
	Chapter 5	Böhm-Bawerks Law of Increased Productivity of Increased Roundaboutness. The Point-Input-Point Output Model	36
	Chapter 6	The Period of Production in more General Models	40
	Chapter 7	Substitution. Switching of Techniques	47
	Chapter 8	The Dynamic Nonsubstitution Theorem. Generalization of the Elasticity of Substitution	53
	Chapter 9	Wicksell Effect. Marginal Productivity of Capital	60
Part III	Fixed Capital		67
	Chapter 1	Machines	67
	Chapter 2	The General Case of Joint Production and a General Nonsubstitution Theorem	72
Part IV	General Equilibrium of Steady States		79
References to the Literature			97

Preface

The following lecture notes were written shortly after I gave a course on capital theory in the winter-semester 1970/71 at the University of Heidelberg. While the general line of the argument is similar to the one in the course, I have modified and added a large number of specific points in the process of writing the English version.

I should like to emphasize the narrow limitations of the material covered in these notes. I have completely concentrated on steady states of stationary and exponentially growing economies, even up to the point where there is the danger of misleading the reader, I have done this for several reasons. Other activities have not left me with a sufficient amount of time to be able to find the unifying principle of analysis and mode of presentation for the dynamic aspects of capital theory which would have made it worthwhile to add a sizeable book to the large body of literature in this field. On the other hand over the last couple of years I have become increasingly aware that some of the results in steady state capital theory (which could be derived without too much mathematical effort) are of relevance in present day discussions about the political role of economic theory and the relative merits of orthodox and radical economics. Also these results seemed not to be known by most of the participants in these discussions. A careful statement of some of these results from a unified point of view seems to be useful, in particular since the mathematical barriers of entry to an understanding are so low.

In writing these notes I wanted to stress the importance of a small number of celebrated and criticised concepts for the understanding of capital theory. These are the Marxian concepts of value and exploitation, Böhm-Bawerk's concept of the period of production, J.B.Clark's principle of synchronization of production and Marshall's principle of substitution. I have tried to develop a logically consistent view of these heuristically important ideas by using certain results of modern growth theory. While it is true that no economy is ever in a steady state I do not think that there exists any other way to draw a simple picture of economics showing how heuristic priciples of interpretation of real economics can be justified by making them precise. That such check by precision is necessary is shown by the results which force us to reject certain heuristic principles. Not all of them keep their appeal if scrutinized sufficiently.

There are at least two important aspects of the process of capital accumulation which cannot be analysed in the context of the static models presented here. One of them is a precise analysis of the payoff between present and future consumption of a society. Orthodox capital theory can state assumptions under which the equivalence of the private and social marginal rate of return on saving follows. This result was analysed and emphasized in particular by Solow. As he has pointed out and as I have reiterated elsewhere it is independent of the answer to one of the by now almost classic red herrings of economic theory: the question whether there exists an aggregate production function with "capital" as one of its arguments. The other specifically dynamic aspect of capital theory is the question of flexibility of a system. The point of view taken in these lecture notes is to reduce the production process to flows of primary inputs and final outputs. This is all right for comparative static analysis. It is misleading for the dynamic analysis of, say, transitions between techniques. Intermediate products, for example steel, can still be used after a switch in techniques of production took place, even though this steel was planned to be used for the former process of production. I disagree therefore with the view of Hicks that Walrasian general equilibrium theory is suited for static analysis and Austrian capital theory for dynamic analysis. I take the opposite view: Austrian capital theory is a good starting point to analyse the time pattern of production and its implications under conditions of tranquility, where transitions between technique do not take place. Walrasian equilibrium theory will have to be used to study these transition problems, because under such conditions intermediate products have to be considered in their own right. They are no longer just manifestations of a certain amount of past labour inputs or future consumption goods.

These lecture notes are a semi-finished product. The references to the literature, which I put into a bibliographical appendix, are incomplete. A number of extensions and corollaries of the results presented here are not contained in these notes, though they ought to be here. I did not find the time to work them out properly. But I hope that, as the presented results stand, they are not only correct but also comprehensible. As an apology I may refer the reader to the law of diminishing marginal returns: it also applies to work done on steady state models in capital theory, and I am anxious to switch to other fields of research.

I should like to mention three groups of people to whom I owe thanks for direct or indirect help in writing these notes. The first group consists of three of my former teachers: Friedrich Lutz, whose lectures in Zürich and whose book "Zinstheorie" convinced me to switch from law to economics and to take capital theory as one of my favourite fields. His influence also made me read Böhm-Bawerk. Gottfried Bombach, who in 1959 encouraged me to pursue my work on growth theory and capital theory, after I had told him a result which was later to be called the "Golden Rule of Accumulation". Edgar Salin, who convinced me to read three volumes of "Das Kapital" in a time when nobody else did and I still had plenty of time to do it.

The second group of people consists of assistants and students in Heidelberg, who endured my lectures and discussed the material with me. They are Felix R. FitzRoy, Martin Hellwig, Hans Gottfried Nutzinger, Wolfgang Rohde, Georg Tolkemitt and Elmar Wolfstetter. I am also indebted to Brigitte Wölm, who was able to take tidy and clear notes of what clearly sometimes must have been a confusing presentation (if not confused), and who was so kind to lend her notes to me.

The third group consists of my friends at MIT, where I stayed for a month in spring 1971 writing down a large part of these notes. I am particularly indebted to Paul Samuelson for extensive discussions last year as well as this year. Comments of Michael Bruno, Frank Hahn, Robert Solow and Joseph Stiglitz were also helpful in revising the first draft. I am indebted to the Ford Foundation which covered my expenses while I was at MIT from February 21 to March 21, 1971.

Part I

Capital Theory without Capital (Preliminaries to Capital Theory)

If we want to understand what we are talking about when we are talking about capital we should have a clear perspective: which phenomena are specifically related to capital and which are not. For that purpose it is useful to state certain results of price theory which are independent of the introduction of the concept of capital. This is the purpose of the first part of these lecture notes.

Chapter 1. The Static Input-Output Model without Substitution

We begin with a somewhat selective treatment of Input Output analysis. We assume an economy with n producible goods. In order to produce one unit of good j the economy needs a_{ij} units of good i (for i=1,...n) as input. Thus if industry j (which produces good j) wants to produce x_j units of output it must receive $a_{1j} x_j$ units as inputs from industry 1, $a_{2j} x_j$ units as inputs from industry 2 and so on. The set of input-output ratios a_{ij} form an n times n matrix which we call A. All a_{ij} are nonnegative, quite a few of them will probably be zero. There is one additional commodity, called "labour". It's specific characteristic is that it cannot be produced in the usual sense of the word. We assign the index zero to this commodity. Thus for every j we have an input output ratio a_{oj} which tells us how much labour per unit of output is necessary in industry j. The vector $(a_{o1}, a_{o2}, \ldots a_{on})$ is denoted by a_o.

Let $x = (x_1 \ldots x_n)$ be the vector of the output quantities in the different industries. Let y_i be the quantity of good i which is used up in the economy as an input for productive purpose. We then have the following system of equations

$$y_1 = a_{11} x_1 + a_{12} x_2 + \cdots \cdots a_{1n} x_n$$
$$\vdots$$
$$y_n = a_{n1} x_1 + \cdots \cdots \cdots a_{nn} x_n$$

or written in matrix form
$$y = Ax$$

There arises now the following intersting question. Are the outputs produced sufficient to replace the inputs which have been used up in the process of producing these outputs? Or: under which condition is $y \leq x$? The purpose of production is the supply of commodities for consumption. Let $c = (c_1, c_2, \ldots c_n)$ be the vector of commodities which the productive system can deliver to the outside world after the inputs of the production process have been replaced. Then we have $c = x - y$. The question above is therefore identical to the question: under which conditions is the consumption vector c nonnegative? We write

$$c = x - y = x - Ax = Ix - Ax = (I - A) x$$

where I stands for the identy matrix

$$\begin{pmatrix} 1 & & & & & & \\ & 1 & & & & & \\ & & 1 & & 0 & & \\ & & & 1 & & & \\ & & & & \ddots & & \\ & 0 & & & & \ddots & \\ & & & & & & 1 \\ & & & & & & & 1 \end{pmatrix}$$

which maps every vector x into itself. We now turn the problem around. Given a certain consumption vector $c \geq 0$. Which production vector x is required, if c is to be made possible. Mathematically we have to solve the system of equations

$$(I - A) x = c$$

for the unknowns x. In the case that $(I - A)$ is nonsingular there exists $(I - A)^{-1}$ and we get

$$x = (I - A)^{-1}(I - A) x = (I - A)^{-1} c$$

But this is not sufficient, since x must be a nonnegative solution. Production cannot be negative. There exists a simple mathematical condition for x to be nonnegative. Starting from the equation $c = (I-A)x$ we can write for any integer m

$$(I + A + A^2 + \ldots A^m) c =$$
$$(I + A + A^2 + \ldots A^m) x$$
$$-(A + A^2 + A^3 + \ldots A^{m+1}) x =$$
$$= (I - A^{m+1}) x.$$ But since A^{m+1} is the product of $m + 1$ nonnegative matrices (namely A) it is nonnegative itself and hence, if $x > 0$ we get $$x > (I - A^{m+1}) x = (I + A + \ldots A^m) c$$
for every m. If $I + A + \ldots A^m$ does not converge for increasing

m to a finite matrix the condition just stated cannot hold for every m and hence x is not nonnegative. For x to be nonnegative the convergence of
$$\sum_{k=0}^{m} A^k$$
for increasing m is a necessary condition. But this condition is also sufficient. If $\lim_{m \to \infty} \sum_{k=0}^{m} A^k$ exists it is given by $(I-A)^{-1}$. For, then we have
$$\sum_{k=0}^{\infty} A^k (I - A) = \sum_{k=0}^{\infty} A^k - \sum_{k=1}^{\infty} A^k = I$$
which proves that $\sum_{k=0}^{\infty} A^k$ is the inverse of $(I - A)$. This shows that $(I - A)^{-1}$ is nonnegative and hence $x \geq 0$.

There is an economic interpretation of this result. For this purpose we define as inputs of the first order the vector
$$y^1 = Ac$$
These are the inputs necessary for the direct production of the consumption goods. By the inputs of the second order we mean those inputs necessary to replace or reproduce the inputs of the first order
$$y^2 = Ay^1 = A \cdot Ac = A^2 c$$
In general: the inputs of the k - th order, y^k, are the inputs necessary to replace by production the inputs of k - 1 - th order. Now it is easy to see that
$$y^k = A^k c$$
The total inputs y that have to be replaced are then
$$y = y^1 + y^2 + \ldots \ldots \ldots =$$
$$= Ac + A^2 c + A^3 c + \ldots \ldots \ldots$$
$$= (A + A^2 + \ldots \ldots \ldots) c$$
Thus the convergence of the sequence
$A + A^2 + \ldots \ldots$ is a necessary and sufficient condition for the total inputs to be finite. Each term in this sum stands for the inputs of a certain order.

A system which is able to replace it's inputs from it's output may be called productive. A technology characterized by the matrix A of input output ratios can provide a productive system if and only if the sum
$$\sum_{k=0}^{\infty} A^k$$
is finite.

Note the following: Take any two consumption vectors c^1 and c^2. There exists an economically meaningful production vector x supporting the consumption vector in either case or in **neither** case. The answer to this question does not depend on the properties of c, but only on the properties of A.

So far we have neglected the labour inputs. How much labour is necessary for the production system? If we call this quantity L we have

$$L = a_{o1} x_1 + a_{o2} x_2 + \ldots \ldots a_{on} x_n$$

or

$$L = a_o x = a_o (I - A)^{-1} c.$$

It is an old tradition in economics to ask how much labour is contained in one unit of a given commodity. The answer can be given by the formula above. If you increase component i of the vector c by one unit the total labour requirement goes up by an amount equal to the i - th component of the vector $a (I - A)^{-1}$ Hence this vector is the vector of the per unit labour content of the final products. It is what Marx calls "socially necessary labour time" for the production of the different commodities in the production of the different commodities in the economy.

We can derive the per unit labour content in a different way. Let z_i be the labour content of good i. Then the following equation must hold

$$z_j = a_{oj} + \sum_{i=1}^{n} a_{ij} z_i$$

In producing one unit of good j a_{oj} units of labour are used up directly. In addition for each i a_{ij} units of good i are used up which embody $a_{ij} z_i$ units labour. Hence the direct and indirect amount of labour is given by the equation above. In matrix form this equation reads

$$z = a_o + z A$$

from which follows

$$z (I - A) = a_o$$
$$z = a_o (I - A)^{-1}$$

It is clear that an economically meaningful solution of this system of equations requires z to be nonnegative. In a similar way as was done above for the system of equations $x = (I - A)^{-1} c$ we can show that the convergence of $\sum_{k=o}^{\infty} A^k$ is a necessary and sufficient condition for z to be nonnegative. Thus we obtain the result: The specific labour content of a commodity is a meaningful concept if and only if the production technology allows the system to be productive. Prices in such a system are proportional to the specific labour contents if we require prices to reflect costs of production. For then the price equations are

$$p_j = wa_{oj} + \sum a_{ij} p_i \quad j = 1, \ldots n$$

or in matrix notation

$$p = wa_o + pA$$

where w is the wage rate. The solution is

$$p = wa_o (I - A)^{-1} = wz$$

This is in accordance with the labour theory of value which says that the exchange rate of goods is given by the ratio of their specific labour content. Thus equilibrium prices exist if and only if the system is productive. Let us note at last for future reference that we can solve the above price equations by an iterative method analogous to the distinction into inputs of first order, second order third order etc. which we have introduced earlier. We compute recursively the following price vectors $p^o, p^1, p^2, \ldots$ by putting

$$p^o = 0, \quad p^1 = wa_o + p^o A = wa_o$$

$$p^2 = wa_o + p^1 A \quad \text{or in general}$$

$$p^t = wa_o + p^{t-1} A$$

which basically means the t-th price vector is equal to the cost of production of the goods, given that prices are equal to p^{t-1}. Clearly we can prove by induction

$$p^t = wa_o (I + A + \ldots + A^{t-1})$$

and hence

$$\lim_{t \to \infty} p^t = wa_o (I + A + \ldots) =$$

$$= wa_o (I - A)^{-1} = p$$

Thus this interative computation process converges. Indeed under not very unrealistic conditions it may be a good and efficient way of approximately computing the equilibrium prices. We also observe that this iterative process of computation has the property of converging monotonically.

Chapter 2. The Static Input-Output Model with Substitution

We are interested in the theory of equilibrium prices, if the industries are able to choose among different methods of production so that with a changing price structure of inputs they are able to substitute one production technique by another. For any given industry j we can stipulate a production function $x_j = x_j(y_{oj}, y_{1j}, \ldots y_{nj})$ relating the output producible to the inputs available which in a natural extension of our notation are denoted by the vector $y_{oj}, \ldots y_{nj}$.

This production function can be derived from the set of available production techniques. Given perfect divisibility of inputs and outputs and given perfect multipliability of the production methods the production function is linear homogeneous and concave. We also assume continuity.

Given such production functions we can derive cost functions and, since we have constant returns to scale unit cost functions which are independent of the quatity of output. Shepard in his by now classic book, Production Functions and Cost Functions has shown how to derive one from the other, let $\phi_j(p,w)$ be the unit cost of producing good j, given commodity prices p and the wage rate w. This unit cost function fulfills the equation

$$\phi_j(p,w) = w\, a_{oj}(p,w) + p\, a^j(p,w)$$

where $a_{oj}(p,w)$ is the labour input per unit of output and $a^j(p,w)$ is the vector of commodity inputs per unit of output. Given substitutability these coefficients depend on the prices of inputs.

We now instroduce the assumption of potential productivity of the system. That is we assume there is available to the economy a matrix $\bar{A}$ of input output ratios such that $\sum_{k=0}^{\infty} \bar{A}^k$ is finite. This implies for every industry j is available a vector $(\bar{a}_{oj}, \bar{a}_{1j}, \ldots \bar{a}_{nj})$ of input output ratios such that the components $(\bar{a}_{1j}, \bar{a}_{2j} \ldots \bar{a}_{nj})$ are the j-th column of matrix $\bar{A}$. This assumption is simply the equivalent for the case with substitution of the assumption of a productive system in the case without substitution.

We are interested in the existence of a market equilibrium in this case with substitution. For this purpose we apply an iterative procedure to compute equilibrium prices. If this iterative procedure converges the existence of equilibrium prices is established. We fix $w > 0$. It is a constant in what follows. We put $p^0 = 0$ and $p_j^{t+1} = \phi_j(p^t, w)$ or in vector notation $p^{t+1} = \phi(p^t, w)$

where ϕ is the vector of unit costs. Now note the following inequality. If the production methods corresponding to $(\bar{a}_{oj}, \bar{a}_{1j}, \ldots \bar{a}_{nj})$ are applied the cost of production for given input prices cannot be lower

than the unit costs (since the latter give the cost minimum among all available methods of production). Hence
$$\phi_j(p,w) \leq w\bar{a}_{oj} + \sum_{i=1}^{n} p_i \bar{a}_{ij},$$
or in vector notation
$$\phi(p,w) \leq w\bar{a}_o + p\bar{A}$$

Now we prove that p^t is monotonically nondecreasing. It is known that unit cost is a nondecreasing function of input prices. Hence we can proceed by induction. Clearly $p^1 = \phi(0,w) \geq 0 = p^o$.
If now $p^{t-1} \leq p^t$ then
$$p^{t+1} = \phi(p^t,w) \geq \phi(p^{t-1},w) = p^t$$
which proves the monotonicity using the monotonicity of the unit cost function in prices. If we now can prove that the sequence p^t is bounded from above then convergence of the sequence follows from it's monotonicity. For this purpose we construct the auxiliary sequence r^t defined by $r^o = o$ and $r^{t+1} = w\bar{a}_o + r^t\bar{A}$. Hence we have $r^t = w\bar{a}_o(I + \bar{A} + \ldots \bar{A}^{t-1})$ hence by assumption about $\bar{A}$ we get
$$\lim_{t\to\infty} r^t = w\bar{a}_o(I - \bar{A})^{-1} \quad \text{and}$$
$$r^t \leq w\bar{a}_o(I - \bar{A})^{-1}$$

Now we show by induction $p^t \leq r^t$. For $t = o$ we have $p^o = r^o = 0$ and the inequality is fulfilled. If $p^{t-1} \leq r^{t-1}$ we can write
$$p^t = \phi(p^{t-1},w) \leq w\bar{a}_o + p^{t-1}\bar{A} \leq w\bar{a}_o + r^{t-1}\bar{A} = r^t$$
which proves the inequality. But putting this together implies $p^t \leq r^t \leq wa_o(I - \bar{A})^{-1}$ and hence p^t is bounded above and thus converges to some value p^*. Continuity of the unit cost function ensures that at the point of convergence the equation
$$p^* = \phi(p^*, w)$$
is fulfilled.

After the proof of existence of an equilibrium price vector we show that there exists only one such equilibrium price vector. To simplify the proof we assume that $a_{oj} > o$ for every j and every available production technique. This implies that the unit cost function $\phi_j(p,w)$ is a strictly increasing function of w.

<u>Proof:</u> Let p^1 and p^2 be two equilibrium price vectors. Choose the index k in such a way that $\lambda_k = \dfrac{p_k^2}{p_k^1} = \max_i \dfrac{p_i^2}{p_i^1}$. Then by the linear homogeneity of the unit cost function we have

$p_k^2 = \lambda_k p_k^1 = \phi_k(\lambda_k p^1, \lambda_k w) \geq \phi_k(p^2, \lambda_k w) > \phi_k(p^2, w)$, if $\lambda_k > 1$ since by assumption the unit cost function is a strict monotonic function of the wage rate. Hence $p_k^2 > p_k^2$ which is a contradition, hence $\lambda_k \leq 1$ which implies $p_2 \leq p_1$. In a symmetric way we prove $p_1 \leq p_2$ and therefore $p_2 = p_1$.

The total labour requirement to produce any given netoutput vector c is given by $\frac{1}{w}(p^* c)$ where p^* is the unique equilibrium price vector.

Proof: Let a_o and A be any available productive input output coefficients. If they are applied we get $x = (I - A)^{-1} c$ and the labour requirement L is $L = a_o (I - A)^{-1} c$. By the cost minimizing property of the unit cost functions we get for the equilibrium prices p^*

$w a_o + p^* A \geq p^*$ or $w a_o \geq p^* (I - A)$ or, since A is assumed to be productive and hence $(I - A)^{-1} \geq o$ $w a_o (I - A)^{-1} \geq p^*$ which implies $L = a_o (I - A)^{-1} c \geq \frac{1}{w}(p^* c)$. On the other hand, if we take the input output ratios which are valid in equilibrium we have

$$p^* = a_o^* w + p^* A^*$$

hence
$$w a_o^* (I - A^*)^{-1} = p^*$$

hence
$$L^* = a_o^* (I - A^*)^{-1} c = \frac{1}{w}(p^* c)$$

The optimum Input Output ratios (which minimize the labour requirements) are the ratios which are selected under equilibrium conditions. They are independent of c. This last property is the so called Nonsubstitution theorem of Arrow, Georgescu-Roegen and Samuelson. It is important, since it says that under conditions of a single nonproducible input the equilibrium prices of all commodities do not depend on the structure of final demand but only on the production technologies available. The choice of techniques problem can be completely separated from the problem of finding the correct composition of output. Let us also emphasize that the labour theory of value is valid with or without the possibility of substitution.

Chapter 3. The Static Input-Output Model with more than One Nonproducible Factor of Production

There is no mathematical difficulty to extend the model to more than one nonproducible (original) input. Let there be r original inputs. The number of input output ratios per industry is then r + n. Again we can define production functions

$$x_j = x_j(l_{1j}, \ldots l_{rj}, y_{1j}, \ldots y_{nj})$$

where the l_{kj} represent direct original inputs in the j-th industry. Let us call b_{kj} the input output ratio of original input k and output j. Let $B = (b_{kj})$ be the r times n matrix of these input output ratios. Let w be the vector of prices of the original inputs. We then have unit cost functions $\phi_j(w, p)$ which form a system of equations

$$p = \phi(w, p)$$

whose solution p^* determines the equilibrium prices. In a similar manner as was done above we can show existence and uniqueness of such an equilibrium price vector p^* for given w. The function $p^*(w)$ determines unit costs of the products as a function of the wages of original inputs. To such a unit cost function $p_j^*(w)$ for the j-th produced commodity corresponds a linear homogeneous "production function" $c_j(l_{1j}, \ldots l_{rj})$ in term of the original inputs only. This "net" production (net of intermediate products) is what from the point of view of the economy as a whole we are interested in. It is an obvious generalization of the concept of labour content of a commodity. Such a net production function can also be computed directly from the production functions in the different industries; but such a computation is not easier than the computation of the unit cost function $p_j^*(w)$ and the computation of the netproduction function from it.

It is well known that the independence of prices from final demand breaks down as soon as we have more than one original factor. There is no a priori principle which could determine the relative wages $w_1, w_2, \ldots w_r$ of the different original factors. They have to be determined in the market. If for example the total supply of the original factors $L_1, L_2, \ldots L_r$ is fixed then their relative prices are fixed by the demand functions for them. But these derived demand functions depend on the final demand for consumption goods. If demand is high for such consumption goods whose production (directly and via the intermediate products) uses factor 1 in large quantities then the equilibrium price of this factor will be high. Given a different demand structure the equilibrium price of factor 1 may be lower (say relative to the equilibrium price of factor 2). But this implies that also the methods of production will be influenced by the structure of final demand. If factor 1 intensive products are in high demand and therefore the equilibrium price of factor 1 is high, firms will use methods of production which save on factor 1 inputs. The situation is different, when the equilibrium price of factor 1 is low. Given any net production function $c_j(\ell_{1j}, \ell_{2j})$ with two original inputs we can construct a factor price frontier. We use for this purpose the unit cost function $p_j^*(\bar{w}_1, \bar{w}_2)$ where $\bar{w}_1$ and $\bar{w}_2$ are the money wage rates. The real wage rate

$$w_1 = \frac{\bar{w}_1}{p_j^*}, \quad w_2 = \frac{\bar{w}_2}{p_j^*}$$

can be computed. Since p_j^* is a linear homogeneous function of $\bar{w}_1$ and $\bar{w}_2$, w_1 and w_2 are completely determined after the ratio of the wage rates is fixed. By putting $p_j^* = 1$ we can determine w_2 as a function of w_1 from the equation

$$1 = p_j^*(w_1, w_2)$$

This function $w_2(w_1)$ is called the factor price frontier. This factor price frontier is of course closely related to the production function. Thus it's slope is given by the following computation. Differentiability assumed we know that the slope of the unit isoquant corresponding to the production function is given by the cost minimization condition

$$\frac{dg_{1j}}{dg_{2j}} = -\frac{w_2}{w_1}$$

where $g_{1j} = \frac{l_{1j}}{c_j}$ and $g_{2j} = \frac{l_{2j}}{c_j}$

are the input output ratios of the net production function. Putting unit cost equal to unity (the good j is the numeraire in which the real wage rates are expressed), we have

$$1 = p_j^* = g_{1j} w_1 + g_{2j} w_2$$

Total differentiation yields

$$0 = g_{1j} dw_1 + w_1 dg_{1j} + g_{2j} dw_2 + w_2 dg_{2j}$$

This together with the cost minimization condition yields

$$0 = g_{1j} dw_1 + g_{2j} dw_2$$

or

$$\frac{dw_2}{dw_1} = -\frac{g_{1j}}{g_{2j}}$$

The curvature of the isoquant is determined by the elasticity of substitution

$$\sigma = \frac{d \log \frac{g_{1j}}{g_{2j}}}{d \log \frac{w_2}{w_2}} = \frac{d \log \frac{g_{1j}}{g_{2j}}}{d \log | \text{slope of isoquant}|}$$

In a similar way the curvature of the factor price frontier characterized by

$$\sigma' = \frac{d \log \frac{w_1}{w_2}}{d \log | \text{slope of fpf}|} = \frac{d \log \frac{w_1}{w_2}}{d \log \frac{g_{2j}}{g_{1j}}} =$$

$$= \frac{d \log \frac{w_2}{w_1}}{d \log \frac{g_{1j}}{g_{2j}}} = \frac{1}{\sigma}$$

Thus the two indices of curvature σ and σ' are reciprocal. The more curvature there is in the isoquant (the lower the value of σ) the less curvature there is in the factor price frontier.

To obtain a graphical representation we can represent every technique of production by a straight line in the w_1, w_2 diagram. This line represents the combinations of w_1 and w_2 which can be paid to the original factors of production, given that this technique of production is used. The slope of this line represents ratio of the intensities with which the two original factors are used (directly and indirectly). If we draw the different lines corresponding to different techniques of production then the relevant factor price is the upper envelope of all these lines. For every given value of w_1 the technique is chosen which maximizes the wage of the other factor of production (and vice versa)

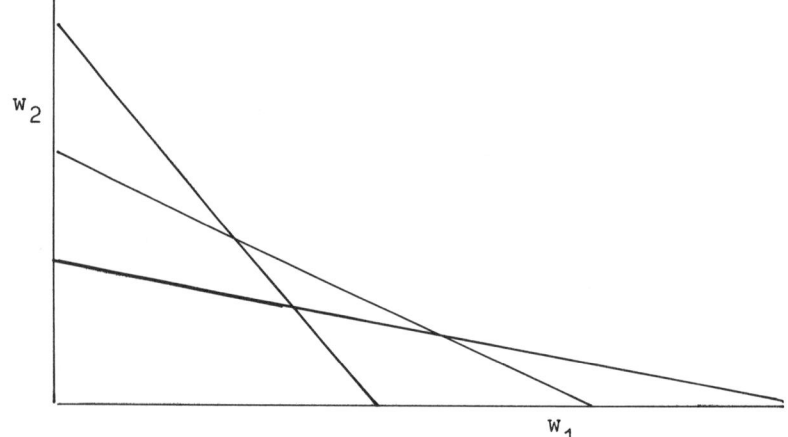

Part II

Circulating Capital

Chapter 1. A One Sector Model

We now want to introduce the time dimension into the production process explicitely. Inputs have to be made available before the outputs are available. We first consider a very simple model with only one producible commodity and one nonproducible good (called labour). To produce one unit of the commodity we need a units of this commodity as input ($0 < a < 1$) and a_o units of labour input. Both inputs have to be available one period before the availability of the output. But we assume that the wage is paid to workers only after the output has become available. Hence there is no interest cost on wage payments. If the price of the commodity is p, if the nominal wage rate is $\bar{w}$ and if the interest rate is r we have the unit cost equation

$$p = a_o \bar{w} + (1+r) ap$$

or

$$p = \frac{a_o \bar{w}}{1-(1+r)a}$$

The real wage rate $w = \frac{\bar{w}}{p}$ in terms of the commodity is

$$w = \frac{\bar{w}}{\frac{a_o \bar{w}}{1-(1+r)a}} = \frac{1 - (1+r) a}{a_o}$$

The real wage rate is a linear downward sloping function of the rate of interest. It reminds

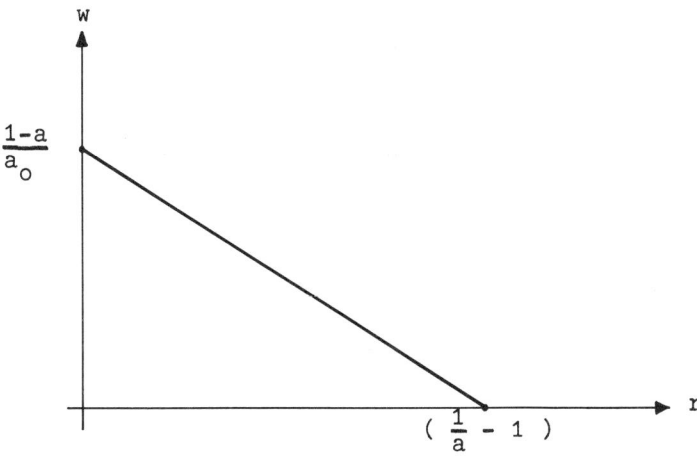

one of the factor price frontier. The slope is given by $-\frac{a}{a_o}$. On a macroeconomic level we assume that labour supply L grows at a rate g. The total volume of production under conditions of full employment of labour is then given for time t as (L_t is the amount of labour paid at time t)

$$x_t = \frac{1}{a_o} L_t$$

Commodity inputs will then have to be at time t - 1

$$y_{t-1} = a x_t$$

Since $x_{t+1} = (1+g) x_t$, we then have $y_t = (1+g) y_{t-1} = (1+g) a x_t$

Total consumption $\bar{c}_t$ is then

$$\bar{c}_t = x_t - y_t = x_t - (1+g) a x_t = x_t (1-(1+g)a) = L_t \frac{1-(1+g)a}{a_o}$$

Consumption per head c is

$$c = \frac{\bar{c}_t}{L_t} = \frac{1 - (1+g)a}{a_o}$$

The relation between consumption per head and the rate of growth is mathematically identical to the relation between the real wage rate and the rate of interest.

We are interested to find out how much capital or wealth is in the economy at any given moment. Let V be the value of the stock of commodities in the economy. The stock must grow at the rate g and hence net investment $I = g V$. Net national product Q is then $Q = I + \bar{c} = g V + \bar{c} = g V + c L = (g v + c) L$, where v is the value per worker. On the other hand we must have $Q = r V + w L = (r v + w) L$. Hence

$$g v + c = r v + w$$

or, if $r \neq g$

$$v = \frac{c - w}{r - g}$$

Since c and w can be determined as functions of v and g we compute

$$v = \frac{1 - (1+g) a - (1-(1+r)a)}{r - g} \cdot \frac{1}{a_o} = \frac{a}{a_o} \cdot \frac{r-g}{r-g} = \frac{a}{a_o}$$

v is then the slope of the wage-interest curve and the consumption-growth curve.

We now introduce substitution. Let there be a curve $a = \psi(a_o)$ along which firms can select one point which then determines the two input output coefficients. We assume $\psi(a_o)$ to be differentiable - which is not a very important assumption - and

$$\psi'(a_o) < 0, \quad \psi''(a_o) > 0$$

The choice of technique now depends on input prices. Every technique of production can be represented by a straight line on the r - w - diagram. The slope of the line is equal to the

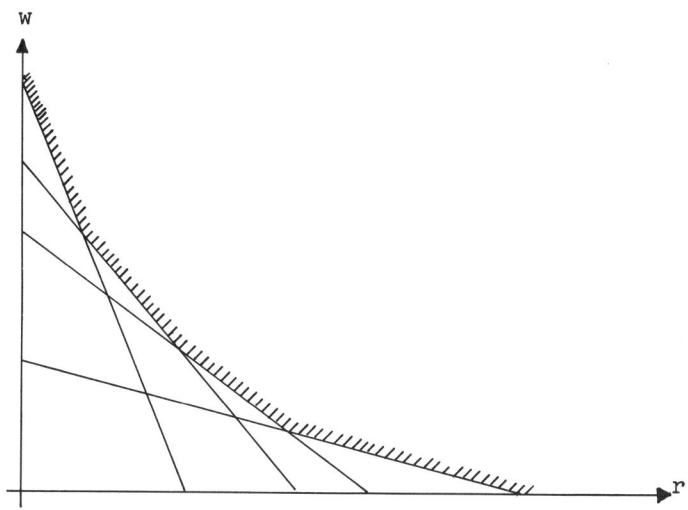

(negative) ratio of inputs $-\frac{a}{a_o}$. For any given wage rate the firm will choose the technique which maximizes the rate of profit and thus now the outer envelope of all lines will be what we call the wage-interest curve of the economy. To put it the other way round. Given a certain interest rate, firms can afford to pay a real wage rate which is equal to the maximum of all wage-interest curves at this interest rat. Demand for labour will be higher than supply until the wage rate has risen to that level. Only the technique(s) which can pay the maximum wage rate will actually be used.

If the isoquant $a = \psi(a_o)$ is differentiable the same is true of the outer envelope of the different wage interest curves. By the envelope theorem the slope of the wage-interest curve must always be

$$\frac{dw}{dr} = -\frac{a}{a_o} = -v$$

where $\frac{a}{a_o}$ refers to the technique which is in use at that point. But since we have for net output per worker $\quad q = rv + w$

we obtain
$$dq = rdv + vdr + dw$$
$$\frac{dq}{dv} = r + v\frac{dr}{dv} + \frac{dw}{dv}$$

Because of $\frac{dw}{dr} = -v$ we have

$$\frac{dw}{dv} = \frac{dw}{dr} \cdot \frac{dr}{dv} = -v\frac{dr}{dv} \quad \text{and hence}$$

$$\frac{dq}{dv} = r + v\frac{dr}{dv} - v\frac{dr}{dv} = r$$

The marginal product of capital is equal to the rate of interest. We are then able to develop, what Samuelson calls a surrogate production function which relates net output per man to capital per man and which has the property that the marginal product of capital is equal to the rate of interest.

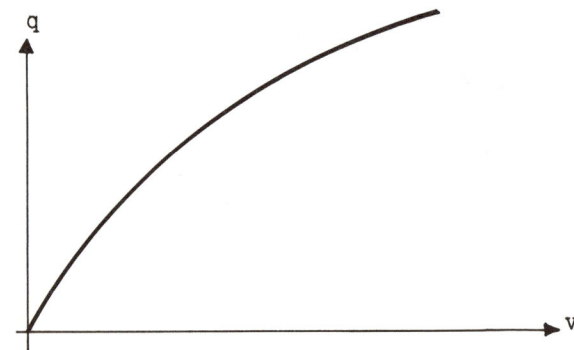

This "production function" is not a technical relationship in the strict sense. The technology has been described in terms of the input output ratios a and a_o and the unit isoquant $a = \psi(a_o)$. But we can treat it, as if it were a technological relationship. Thus for example the Solow-growth model takes such a "production function" and treats it as a technological relationship. Our analysis **here shows** that such a procedure may be legitimate even though the underlying technology is different. But the limits of this procedure will become clear in the next chapter.

Chapter 2. Many Goods, no Substitution

We now return to the many goods case. But we assume that there is only one kind of original input, which we call labour. If workers are paid at the end of the period but all other inputs are paid at the beginning of the period we get the following price equation for good j

$$p_j = a_{oj}\bar{w} + (1+r)\sum_{i=1}^{n} a_{ij} p_i \quad j=1,\ldots n$$

or in matrix notation

$$p = \bar{w} a_o (I - (1-(1+r) A)^{-1}$$

If the system is productive then for sufficiently small r the matrix $(I -(1+r) A)^{-1}$ is nonnegative so that the solution of the price equations makes sense.

In order to derive a relation between the real wage rate and the interest rate we have to define the real wage. For this purpose we take a standard commodity basket $s = (s_1, \ldots, s_n)$. The real wage rate is then defined by the number of standard baskets which one can buy with a given nominal wage rate and at given prices. The price of the standard basket is $p_1 s_1 + p_2 s_2 \ldots p_n s_n = p \cdot s$ and hence the real wage rate is defined to be

$$w = \frac{\bar{w}}{p\,s}$$

where $\bar{w}$ is the nominal wage rate. Then we get

$$w = \frac{\bar{w}}{\bar{w} a_o (I -(1+r) A)^{-1} s} = \frac{1}{a_o (I-(1+r) A)^{-1} s}$$

If we look at an exponentially growing economy with this technology we have for the vector of inputs at time t

$$y^t = (1+g) y^{t-1} = (1+g) A x^t$$

hence for the vector of total consumption

$$\bar{c} = x - y = (I - (1+g) A) x$$

or, for any given vector $\bar{c}$ we find the production vector

$$x = (I - (1+g) A)^{-1} \bar{c}$$

The consumption level per head is defined in analogy to the real wage rate. We assume that the vector $\bar{c}$ is proportional to the standard basket s

$$\bar{c} = \lambda s$$

where λ is some skalar. The level of consumption per worker (per head) is then defined to be the number of commodity baskets per head which is available for consumptive purposes in the economy. We call it c, which is a skalar. We have

$$c = \frac{\lambda}{L}$$

But we have an equation for L

$$L = a_o x = a_o (I -(1+g) A)^{-1} \bar{c} =$$
$$= a_o (I -(1+g) A^{-1}) \lambda s$$

Dividing this equation by L yields

$$1 = a_0 (I - (1+g) A)^{-1} s c \quad \text{or}$$

$$c = \frac{1}{a_0 (I - (1+g) A)^{-1} s}$$

We observe the following important duality property: The dependence of c on g has the same mathematical form as the dependence of the real wage rate on the interest rate. Thus the wage-interest curve has a dual interpretation as the consumption-growth curve of an economy using the production technique in question.

It is perhaps worthwhile to make a remark on Marxian value theory in this context. As is well known there is a difference between value and price in the Marxian system. The value of a commodity is proportional to the specific labour content of the commodity. But Marx and his successors know that in a capitalistic economy goods are traded at prices which are not necessarily equal to the values. Equality of prices and values obtains only (if one disregard technical progress for this exercise to which we will turn later in a similar context), if the rate of interest i . e . the degree of exploitation is zero. "Bourgeois" economists have frequently asked the critical question: what is the use of a concept of value as distinct from the concept of price if you want to understand the functioning of the capitalistic system? We cannot discuss this question here: let us only note that the Marxian concept of exploitation is derived from value theory and could not be derived in a similar way from the Marxian price theory. In fact the price theory (of Volume III of Das Kapital) presupposes the theory of exploitation (of Volume I of Das Kapital). Let us grant for the purpose of the argument that it makes sense to have a theory of value as distinct from a theory of price.

The next question then is this: is the specific Marxian definition of value the appropriate one? What are the criteria from which to derive an appropriate concept of value? Values for Marxian theory are the form in which in a capitalistic system the social costs of production of commodities appear. The labour theory of value says that the value of a commodity is proportional to the labour time <u>socially necessary</u> to produce it. While values may be something specific to capitalism we can compute the socially necessary labour time in other systems too, say in a rationally organized socialist system. In such a system, according to Engels there exists a production plan and "the utilities (in German: "Nutzeffekte") of the different useful objects, weighed against each other and against the quantities of labour necessary to produce them will determine the plan". In other words one of the main purposes of the plan in a socialist economy is to allocate the quantities of labour in such a way that they yield a maximum of use value. It is the idea that the labour content of a product represents it's opportunity costs of production. Instead of producing it society could have produced any other thing requiring the same amount of labour. A socialist society would therefore value each product according to it's socially necessary labour time.

Using this unit of account the total "value" (value here is not necessarily exchange value, since no market relations need exist) of final products of a society with given expenditure of labour is the same whatever the specific product mix of these final output may be. Given the decision about the composition of the basket of final products the planners determine the quantities of intermediate products that have to be produced according to the technological conditions of the economy.

Let us now go back to our model and try out this labour unit of account. Let π_1 be the "value" of good 1 ..... and let π be the vector $(\pi_1, \ldots, \pi_n)$. Then it is required that in an equilibrium system with a given supply of labour the total value of final products be the same and idependent of the composition of the vector of final products which we called $\bar{c}$. Now we have the equation

$$L = a_0 (I - (1+g) A)^{-1} \bar{c}$$

If we put $\pi = a_0 (I - (1+g) A)^{-1}$ then the "value" of $\bar{c}$ (val) is given by

$$val = \pi \bar{c} = L$$

and hence for given L it is independent of the specific structure of $\bar{c}$. Now observe that the price equation is given by

$$p(r) = \bar{w} a_0 (I - (1+r) A)^{-1}$$

Hence the value vector π can be identified with

$$\pi = \frac{1}{\bar{w}} p(g)$$

The values of commodities are proportional to their prices which would prevail in a market system if the interest rate would be equal to the rate of growth.

This result is not consistent with the Marxian definition of value. This would **only** be the case, if the rate of growth of the system were zero. We have to keep in mind that the Marxian definition of value was developed in a time in which there did not yet exist a well developed body of knowledge of growth economics. Thus he and Engels implicitly assumed a stationary economy when they believed that the specific labour content of a commodity is the right indicator of social opportunity costs in producing this commodity. They did not ralize that one has to weigh labour units according to the date of their availability and that this weighting system depends on the rate of growth of the system. - It is probably easier to understand the problems involved, if we turn to the method of computing the flow of labour inputs which are necessary for the production of final products.

Chapter 3. Dated Labour Inputs and the Theory of Value and Exploitation

If we want to produce one unit of good j at time zero a_{oj} units of labour have to be available at time -1 and have to be paid at time zero. In addition the vector $y^{1j} = (a_{1j}, \ldots, a_{nj})$ has to be available at time -1. In order to produce this vector $a_{o1}a_{1j} + a_{o2}a_{2j} + \ldots a_{on}a_{nj} = a_o y^{1j}$ units of labour have to be made available at time -2 (and have to be paid at time -1). In addition the vector of inputs $y^{2j} = Ay^{1j}$ has to be available at time -2. This again requires labour in the amount $a_o y^{2j}$ and so on. We can give a tabular representation of this computation in the following way

commodity inputs	$y^{7j}=Ay^{6j}$	$y^{6j}=Ay^{5j}$	$y^{5j}=Ay^{4j}$	$y^{4j}=Ay^{3j}$	$y^{3j}=Ay^{2j}$	$y^{2j}=Ay^{1j}$	y^{1j}	
. . . .	-7	-6	-5	-4	-3	-2	-1	0 → t

The time series of labour inputs is then (we put the inputs on the time axis according to the payment of wages)

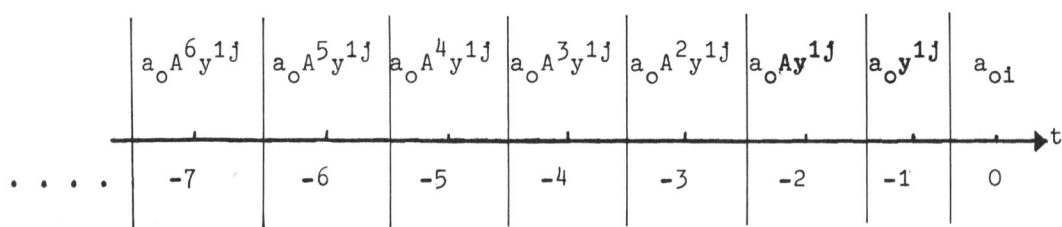

	$a_oA^6y^{1j}$	$a_oA^5y^{1j}$	$a_oA^4y^{1j}$	$a_oA^3y^{1j}$	$a_oA^2y^{1j}$	a_oAy^{1j}	a_oy^{1j}	a_{oi}
. . . .	-7	-6	-5	-4	-3	-2	-1	0 → t

This last sequence shows how the intermediate products can be dissolved into a flow of labour inputs which is a prerequisite of the final output. Let $\alpha_j(t)$ be the labour input necessary at time -t for the production of unit of good j at time zero. Then we have $\alpha_j(o) = a_{oj}$ $\alpha_j(1) = a_o y^{1j}$, in

general:
$$\alpha_j(t) = a_o A^{t-1} y_j^1$$

In a similar way we are able to compute the labour requirements for any commodity basket s. Let us call them $\alpha_s(t)$. Then we have

$$\alpha_s(0) = a_o s, \quad \alpha_s(1) = a_o A s \quad \text{and in general}$$

$$\alpha_s(t) = a_o A^t s$$

The cost of production of any commodity basket s can be understood to be the sum of the present values of the labour costs of the required labour flow of the basket. This cost k_s is then equal to

$$k_s = \bar{w} \sum_{t=0}^{\infty} \alpha_s(t)(1+r)^t =$$

$$= \bar{w} a_o \sum_{t=0}^{\infty} A^t s (1+r)^t = \bar{w} a_o (I - (1+r)A)^{-1} s = ps$$

since we had derived earlier

$$p = \bar{w} a_o (I - (1+r)A)^{-1}$$

That is, we get the correct results for the prices of the commodities if we compute their production costs via the flow of labour requirements.

If we are now in an integrated growing economic system then in any given period of time the economy is as it were working at the production of consumption goods for many future periods simultaneously. The economy is at the same time engaged in the last stage of production of the consumption goods to be available in the coming period, in the last but one stage of production for the consumption goods to be available one period later and so on. That is it synchronizes the production of consumption goods for different future periods. The following table applies to a system which grows at a rate g and gives an impression of the working of this synchronization. (p.24) If we now look at period 0, we see that labour is used in a total amount of

$a_o s c L_o$ (lowest line) + $a_o A s c L_o (1+g)$ (line above)

+ $a_o A^2 s c L_o (1+g)^2 + \ldots$

The total amount of labour used can of course not exceed L_o and thus by dividing through L_o we get the equation

$$1 = \sum_{t=0}^{\infty} a_o A^t s c (1+g)^t = a_o (I - (1+g)A)^{-1} s c$$

which determines the level of c. It is of course the same equation as we

	-5	-4	-3	-2	-1	0	1	2	3	4
			$a_0 A^5 sc L_0 (1+g)^2$	$a_0 A^4 sc L_0 (1+g)^2$	$a_0 A^3 sc L_0 (1+g)^2$	$a_0 A^2 sc L_0 (1+g)^2$	$a_0 A sc L_0 (1+g)^2$	$a_0 sc L_0 (1+g)^2$		
		$a_0 A^5 sc L_0 (1+g)$	$a_0 A^4 sc L_0 (1+g)$	$a_0 A^3 sc L_0 (1+g)$	$a_0 A^2 sc L_0 (1+g)$	$a_0 A sc L_0 (1+g)$	$a_0 sc L_0 (1+g)$			
	$a_0 A^5 sc L_0$	$a_0 A^4 sc L_0$	$a_0 A^3 sc L_0$	$a_0 A^2 sc L_0$	$a_0 A sc L_0$	$a_0 sc L_0$				

Production of consumption goods available at $t=2$

Production of consumption goods available at $t=1$

Production of consumption goods available at $t=0$

had already derived. Our "theory of value" now perhaps becomes clearer. Because we consider steady state situations an additional provision of one unit of consumption good i today implies that we provide $(1+g)$ additional units of good i tomorrow, $(1+g)^2$ additional units of the same good the day after tomorrow and so on. This implies that we have to provide today $a_i(o) + (1+g) a_i(1) + (1+g)^2 a_i(2) + (1+g)^3 a_i(3) + \ldots$ additional units of labour which means a corresponding sacrifice in terms of another consumption good. But this total labour requirement of this additional unit of the consumption good is exactly represented by it's costs of production (for a nominal wage rate $\bar{w}$ equal to one), if the rate of interest at which earlier labour costs are compounded is equal to g, the rate of growth of the system.

Now of course the question is: why should we restrict our attention to steady states only? The answer in this context is threefold. We are interested to give the concept of "value" (as opposed to price) an operational meaning. It is a well known fact in modern theory that relative prices (and not what Marx calls values) are an indicator of the marginal rates of transformation between two consumption goods, if we are just interested in a single trade off between two goods (that is a trade off limited to one period). Thus it must be this steady state trade off between goods which remains for the purpose of justifying the concept of value. Secondly, under conditions of no substitutability in the methods of production the usual case will be that a one period deviation from a steady state situation can only be accomplished by not fully utilizing all available resources (due to bottlenecks in other resources), so that relative prices underrepresent the opportunity costs of additional consumption of some commodity. Thirdly and most importantly: A rational planner must have an independent interest in these steady state **payoffs**, perhaps even a dominating interest in these kinds of payoffs: if he is for example interested in an improvement of the **housing condition of the** population he must calculate the cost of a <u>permanent</u> increase of the supply of square meters of housing space per inhabitant. For this purpose this steady state calculation is exactly what he needs.

The concept of a labour unit of account or "value" as opposed to price may therefore be useful in discussing problems of rational planning. But the value should then be computed by giving the labour inputs of a commodity time dependent weights and thereby taking account of the rate of growth of the system. It should be noted that according to this concept of value, price and value coincide when the rate of interest is equal to the rate of growth which means that the sum of profits on capital and the value of net investments are equal.

This concept of value can of course not replace the role of prices in the planning process. It only applies to steady state comparisons and and in any real planning situation with given initial conditions the dynamic problems of the transition from one state to another are important. In this context the usual prices are indispensable. The distinction between the value concept and the price concept is somewhat similar to the distinction between the Golden Rule of Accumulation and a true dynamic theory of optimal accumulation.

Marxian theory relates the theory of value to the theory of exploitation. The theory of value has to explain how exploitation is possible in a situation in which every agent operates on the basis of free contracts. Marx explains the possibility of exploitation from the fact that the commodity labour power produces more value than corresponds to it's own value. The value of the commodity labour power is equal to the amount of labour necessary to reproduce itself: if this is less than one unit of labour then the surplus of value produced by the commodity labour power over the value of labour is the surplus value which is appropriated by the capitalist, i.e. the owner of the means of production. The degree of exploitation is then defined by the ratio of surplus labour to necessary labour (i.e. labour time necessary to reproduce the labour power). The labour theory of value thus gives the key which connects the distribution of values produced in the economy between the classes with the degree of exploitation in the economy. By the definition of value it is true that the degree of exploitation, e, is

$$e = \frac{\text{surplus labour}}{\text{necessary labour}} = \frac{\text{surplus value}}{\text{necessary value}}$$

This degree of exploitation is not correctly reflected in the distribution of national product as evaluated in market prices and therefore cannot be easily computed from "bourgeois" national accounting statistics. Indeed I shall argue presently that the distribution of income in "bourgeois" terminology is a grossly misleading indicator of the degree of exploitation in the Marxian definition.

Marx discussed at length the difference between prices and values and Marxists who have understood what they call the transformation problem are well aware of the fact that the distribution of national product in market prices correctly reflects the degree of exploitation only if one commodity, namely labour power has a price equal to it's value. Only then and if we have a truly stationary economy the folowing equation holds: share of wages in national income in market prices = value of labour power divided by value produced by labour power. But there is no reason to assume that labour power has a market price equal to it's value. This would only be true if the means of substistence of the workers would sell at their value which presupposes that the "organic composition of capital" of the industries producing the means of subsistence is equal to the economy's average organic composition of capital. There is no reason to assume that this must be so. Thus value computations, i.e. computations in terms of socially necessary labour remain necessary if you wish to keep track of the degree of exploitation.

Let us for the purpose of simplifications assume that the labour force is stationary in our following exercise. A similar analysis can be made under different assumptions such as an exogenously or endogenously growing labour force. We now assume that productivity grows exponentially where for our present purpose it does not matter whether this productivity growth is exogenous or (which is more ralistic and more in the Marxian tradition) endogenously determined by what Marx calls "production of relative surplus value". In terms of our input output system we assume that the labour input vector a_o declines exponentially through time so that

$$a_o(t) = (1+\gamma)^{-t} \bar{a}_o$$

The Marxian values of the commodities, i.e. their specific labour content are then given by $\Pi = (\Pi_1, \ldots \Pi_n)$ with

$$\Pi_j(t) = a_{oj}(t) + \sum_{i=1}^{n} a_{ij} \Pi_i(t-1)$$

or in matrix notation

$$\Pi(t) = a_o(t) + \Pi(t-1) A$$

Now, due to the growth of productivity the value of the commodities declines exponentially through time and we have

$$\Pi(t) = (1+\gamma)^{-1} \Pi(t-1) \quad \text{or}$$
$$\Pi(t-1) = (1+\gamma) \Pi(t)$$

It therefore follows

$$\Pi(t) = (1+\gamma)^{-t} \bar{a}_o + (1+\gamma)\Pi(t) A$$

$$\Pi(t) \left(I - (1+\gamma) A\right) = (1+\gamma)^{-t} \bar{a}_o$$

$$\Pi(t) = (1+\gamma)^{-t} \bar{a}_o \left(I - (1+\gamma) A\right)^{-1}$$

If $z(t)$ is the vector of final products or consumption and if $z(t)$

grows exponentially at rate γ we have the equation

$$x(t) = (I - (1+\gamma)A)^{-1} z(t) = (I - (1+\gamma)A)^{-1}(1+\gamma)^t \bar{z}$$

and the labour requirements are

$$L = a_o(t) x(t) = (1+\gamma)^{-t} \bar{a}_o (I - (1+\gamma)A)^{-1} \bar{z} =$$
$$= \pi(t)(1+\gamma)^t \bar{z} = \pi(\gamma) z(t)$$

The total value of final products is thus equal to L and hence independent of time. The value of wage payments, W and the value of profits (surplus value) S are given by

$$e = \frac{S}{W}$$

$$L = W + S = W(1+e) \quad \text{or} \quad W = \frac{L}{1+e}$$

How can we measure the rate of exploitation empirically in an easy way? We observe that the total value of consumtpion $\pi(t) z(t)$ is equal to L and hence the rate of exploitation can easily be calculated from the formula

$$W = \frac{L}{1+e} = \frac{\pi(t) z(t)}{1+e} \quad \text{or}$$

$$e = \frac{\pi(t) z(t) - W}{W}$$

The rate of exploitation is the difference between the value of consumption and the value of wages divided by the value of wages. If for the sake of simplicity we assume that this ratio is approximately equal to the ratio of the corresponding value in bourgeois terms then the rate of exploitation is simply

$$e = \frac{c - w}{w} = \frac{c}{w} - 1$$

the ratio of consumption per worker to the wage rate minus one. The simplifying assumption just made is in general justified: it is equivalent to the assumption that the "organic composition of capital" of the wage good industries is equal to the "organic composition of capital" of all consumption good industries. But the former are identical with the major part of the latter. Therefore they must have similar "organic compositions of capital".

Clearly the ratio of profits to the wage bill in terms of bourgeois national accounting is a completely misleading indicator of the rate of exploitation. To get a quantitative impression of the relation of the distribution of income in bourgeois terms to the rate of exploitation, assume that - in bourgeois terminology - only capitalists save and let the ratio of savings (or investment) to profits be denoted by α. Then we have national income equations

$$y = c + i = r v + w$$

where i = investment per worker, $r v$ = profits per worker (in bourgois terms). We then have

$$i = \alpha r v$$

and therefore

$$c + \alpha r v = r v + w$$
$$c - w = (1 - \alpha) r v$$

$$e = \frac{c - w}{w} = (1 - \alpha) \frac{r v}{w}$$

The rate of exploitation is $1 - \alpha$ times profits divided by wages in bourgeois terms. A realistic savings ratio of capitalists is 75%. Then $1 - \alpha$ is equal to $\frac{1}{4}$. The ratio of profits to wages in modern economies is about 1:3 (if you count as wages part of the income of the self-employed). Thus the rate of exploitation appears to be about $\frac{1}{12}$. In bourgeois national accounting terms the ratio of profits to wages is $\frac{1}{3}$.

Let us investigate the situation of no exploitation for a moment. No surplus value is produced, workers receive all additional value produced in any given period and spend it on consumption goods. The rate of profit is zero. No accumulation of capital takes place. The prices of the commodities relative to the wage rate coincide with their values

$$\frac{1}{w} p = \pi = (1+\gamma)^{-t} \bar{a}_o (I - (1+\gamma)A)^{-1}$$

The Marxian values indicate the steady state social payoff **between** any two goods and so do the prices. The prices and Marxian values are proportional to what we have called values in **the** model with a growing labour force and no technical progress.

In bourgeois trms we would tell the story as follows. In real terms, i.e. in constant prices, the economy grows at the rate γ. The share of wages in national product equal to the share of consumption in national product. The share of profits is equal to the proportion of national product which is invested. The rate of profit is equal to the rate of growth of the system. The capital stock also grows at the rate γ. This different description of the same process should be kept in mind when the two schools of thought try to understand each other. The "bourgeois" schools of thought like (to take two schools existing today) the MIT School or the Cambridge School tend to reckon in real output i.e. output at constant prices. The Marxian school reckons in Marxian values whence there cannot be a sustained growth of produced values unless total labour time in the economy increases.

If we look at developed capitalist economies of the twentieth century the major part of economic growth is due to the growth of labour productivity and only a comparatively small fraction of growth is due to an increased expenditure of labour time. Thus in Marxian value terms growth is several times smaller than in bourgeois real output terms. As a consequence of this only a small fraction of net investment in bourgeois terms is capital accumulation in Marxian terms. The bulk of it is the conservation of already accumulated constant capital in the form that new means of production **rep**lace the means of production consumed in the process of production. Correspondingly the profits in bourgeois terms, out which the investment is financed, are mainly not realized surplus value but **repre**sent part of the value of the consumed means of production.

In as much as our model of a stationary labour force (in terms of man hours) reflects certain laws of motion (certainly not all important laws of motion) of advanced capitalist countries the Marxian theory of value does indeed give a better picture of the division of labour time between "necessary labour" and "surplus labour" than the bourgeois figures of the distribution of national income do. This must be so , if we properly understand what is meant by the Marxian concepts. But it can also be seen from the time structure of production. We have shown above how one can derive the flow of labour inputs which are necessary to produce a given vector of final outputs. The Marxian theory of value rests on the assumption that such a computation of the socially necessary labour inputs is possible. Now let in our model for every t and every $T > 0$ $L_{tT}(n)$ be the quantity of labour expended at time t for the production of final goods available at time t+T for the consumption by the working class. Let $L_{tT}(s)$ be the quantity of labour expended at time t for the production of final goods available at time t+T for the (nonproductive) consumption by the capitalist class. Then the degree of exploitation e at time t is given by

$$e = \frac{\sum_{T=0}^{\infty} L_{tT}(s)}{\sum_{T=0}^{\infty} L_{tT}(n)}$$

In the "stationary" system which we are considering and which in Marxian terms is a special case of the model of "simple reproduction" we can apply what can be called a fundamental law of synchronization: the de**gree** of exploitation is also reflected in the distribution of the value of

Chapter 4. Dated Labour Inputs and the Period of Production

The Austrian school, in particular Carl Menger, thought of the production process as being a linear process which went through a finite number of stages. In the first (or highest) stage only nonproducible inputs produce "goods of the highest order". In the next stage nonproducible inputs together with goods of the highest order produce goods of the second highest order and so on until in the last stage nonproducible inputs and goods of the second lowest order produce goods of the lowest order which are consumption goods. It is clear that the matrix of input output coefficients has to have a certain structure in order to confirm with Menger's model of production. If you order the indices of the different goods according to the order number of the goods then the matrix A would look like this. Every stage gets,

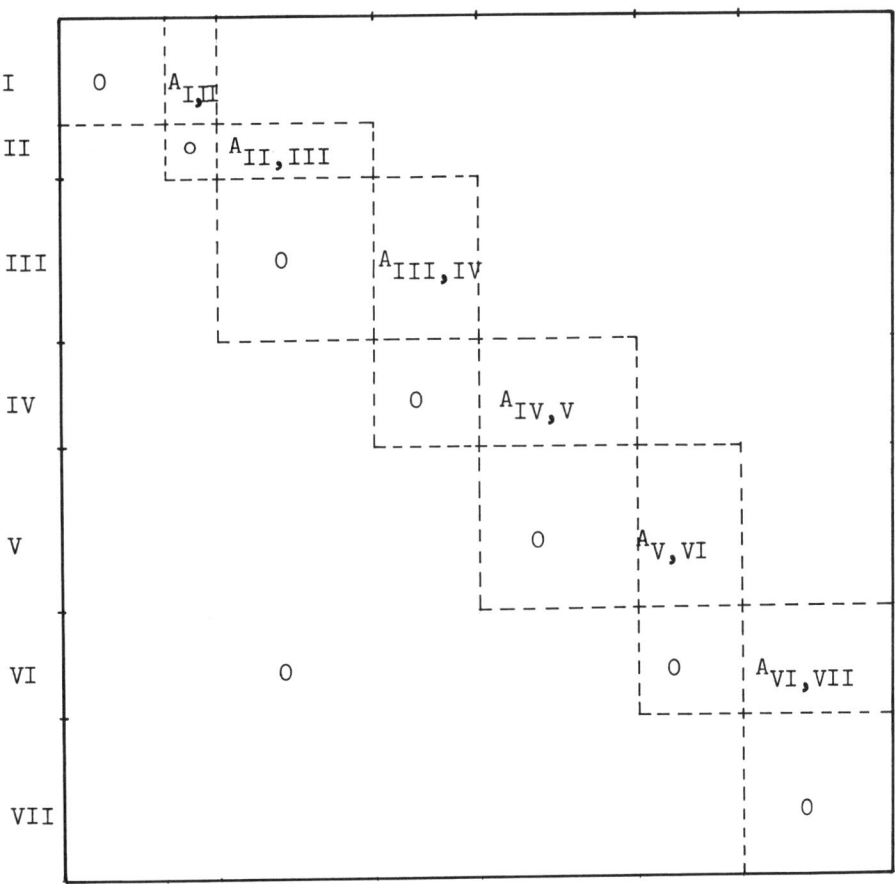

say, a roman number (in the matrix drawn there are seven stages of production). The input output coefficients a_{ij} are zero unless i belongs to a stage one above the stage of j. For every stage J (except the low-final products among the two classes. Indeed the stationarity of the system shows itself in the equations

$$L_{tT}(n) = L_{t'T}(n) = L_T(n)$$
$$L_{tT}(s) = L_{t'T}(s) = L_T(s)$$

for any pair t and t'. The value of final products consumed by the working class at time t_o is of course given by

$$\sum_{t=-\infty}^{t_o} L_{t,t_o-t}(n) = \sum_{t=-\infty}^{t_o} L_{t_o-t}(n) = $$

$$= \sum_{T=0}^{\infty} L_T(n).$$

In a similar way the value of final products consumed by the capitalist class is

$$\sum_{t=-\infty}^{t_o} L_{t,t_o-t}(s) = \sum_{t=-\infty}^{t_o} L_{t_o-t}(s) = \sum_{T=0}^{\infty} L_t(s)$$

which shows that the degree of exploitation is reflected in the value ratio of consumption of capitalists to consumption of workers.

I should like to stress the similarity of the value formula as it was derived above for a socialist economy and the Marxian value formula for the model of a capitalist economy which we discuss just now. The formula for the socialist economy was

$$\Pi = a_o (I - (1+g) A)^{-1}$$

The Marxian formula for the capitalist economy is

$$\Pi = a_o(t) (I + (1+\gamma) A)^{-1}$$

where $a_o(t) = (1+\gamma)^{-t} \bar{a}_o$. In both cases we see that the real rate of interest(i.e. in an accounting system with constant commodity prices) is equal to the rate of growth of the system whenever the prices are proportional of the values. And in both models this rate of interest implies that total labour time is devoted to the production of present and future commodities for the consumption of the working class. We will come back to these considerations in part IV of these lecture notes.

est or last stage) there exists a submatrix $A_{J,J+1}$ containing all the nonzero coefficients linking this stage with the next one. Thus these submatrices are located above (or to the right) of the diagonal submatrices indicating flows of inputs within the same stage which by assumption are nonexistant.

Assuming such a production structure the total production process takes a maximum of m periods, where m is the number of stages. It is not difficult to compute the flow of labour inputs corresponding to any production process leading to some consumption good. It was Böhm-Bawerk who introduced the concept of the average period of production. By this he meant the average time distance between original inputs and the final output. If there are m production stages we can define the average period of production for commodity i

$$T = \frac{\sum_{t=0}^{m-1} \alpha(t) \, t}{\sum_{t=0}^{m-1} \alpha(t)}$$

The importance of this concept lies in the fact that the average period of production is in some way or other related to the quantity of capital that is involved in the production process. Böhm-Bawerk believed that he could directly derive the relative capital intensity from the average period of production. In order to make this plausible let us assume a stationary production system and we shall for the moment assume that the rate of interest is equal to zero. Given the wage rate $\bar{w}$ the value of the product of the earliest stage is equal to $\bar{w} \alpha(m-1)$, the value of the product of the next stage is $\bar{w}(\alpha(m-1) + \alpha(m-2))$ and so on. Now in a stationary system every stage of production is active at the same time, so that the total value of means of production in the system is given by

$$V = \bar{w} \left((\alpha(m-1)) + (\alpha(m-1) + \alpha(m-2)) + \right.$$
$$\left. (\alpha(m-1) + \alpha(m-2) + \alpha(m-3) + \ldots + (\alpha(m-1) + \ldots + \alpha(1)) \right) =$$

$$\bar{w} \sum_{t=0}^{m-1} t \, \alpha(t).$$

If we divide this by the value of net product (or consumption), Q, in the system (which is equal to $\bar{w} \sum_{t=0}^{m-1} \alpha(t)$)

we get

$$\frac{V}{Q} = \frac{\bar{w} \sum_{t=0}^{m-1} t\alpha(t)}{\bar{w} \sum_{t=0}^{m-1} \alpha(t)} = T$$

The capital output ratio in the economy is equal to the average period of production.

This result does of course not depend on the Mengerian structure of production. Several authors (Morgenstern, Knight) have criticized the concept of average period of production on the ground that the production process usually is circular in the sense that some good 1 is an input of good 2 and good 2 is directly or indirectly an input of good 1. In such a case, as can easily be shown the flow of required labour inputs for some final output extends into minus infinity. Thus the production process has no well defined beginning. This was concidered to be an obstacle to the definition of an average period of production. But it need not be one and usually it is not, for the expression

$$T = \frac{\sum_{t=0}^{\infty} \alpha(t) t}{\sum_{t=0}^{\infty} \alpha(t)}$$

usually is finite and hence well defined. In probability theory we are used to probability distributions extending over an infinite range which have a finite expected value. Hence even though historically the concept of an average period of production was developed under the influence of the Menger theory the assumptions of this theory are not necessary.

The real difficulty of Böhm-Bawerks approach to the measurement of capital is that the valuation of a given stock of intermediate products depends on the rate of interest. The capital output ratio is therefore in general a function of the rate of interest. So far we only have shown: capital output ratio and average period of production are equal when the rate of growth and the rate of interest are zero. Böhm-Bawerk circumvented this valuation difficulty by assuming a peculiar kind of computing present values. He applied the principle of simple interest payment instead, what would have been correct, compound interest payment. Thus interest is paid only on those parts of capital which are the direct result of an outlay of labour costs, while those parts of capital which are due to earlier interest payment do not get interest payments. Given this procedure we can compute the costs of production of a commodity

(we drop the index of the commodity)

$$p = \bar{w} \alpha_0 + \bar{w}(1+r)\alpha_1 + \bar{w}(1+2r)\alpha_2 + \bar{w}(1+3r)\alpha_3 + \ldots$$

or

$$p = \bar{w} \sum_{t=0}^{\infty} \alpha_t (1+tr)$$

In a stationary system net output per worker (in physical units) must be equal to

$$c = \frac{1}{\sum_{t=0}^{\infty} \alpha_t}$$

The value of net output per worker is pc

$$pc = \bar{w} \frac{\sum \alpha_t (1+tr)}{\sum \alpha_t}$$

This value of net output is distributed between workers and capitalists and we have

$$pc = \bar{w} + rv$$

where v is the interest earning part of capital. We then can compute

$$rv = pc - \bar{w} = \bar{w} \left(\frac{\sum \alpha_t (1+tr)}{\sum \alpha_t} - 1 \right) = \bar{w} r \frac{\sum \alpha_t t}{\sum \alpha_t}$$

and hence

$$\frac{v}{\bar{w}} = \frac{\sum \alpha_t t}{\sum \alpha_t} = T$$

The ratio of interest earning capital v to the wage bill is given by the average period of production. But it should be clear that this is not total wealth in the economy. There is additional wealth which does not earn interest. Böhm-Bawerk called capital the subsistence fund, **by which** he meant: since labour has to be expended long before the final product **accrues** there must be some funds out which worker can be fed before the product is available. This is the subsistence funds which allows roundabout methods of production that is methods of production in which final output accrues only with a substantial time lag after the inputs. But it is important to see that this subsistence fund is nothing but the intermediate products of processes of production which are under way. The subsistence fund does not consist of a great heap of goods ready for consumption, but it is embodied in intermediate products which will slowly turn into consumption goods. Here it is important to realise that different processes of production which at any given moment of time are in different stages of maturity are synchronized properly so that a steady flow of consumption goods is supplied even though any given process of production is not able in itself to provide it's final products in an evenly distributed manner. This principle of synchronization is **important** if the stock of intermediate products is to serve as a Böhm-Bawerkian fund of subsistence.

Chapter 5. Böhm-Bawerks Law of Increased Productivity of Increased Round**aboutness**. The Point-Input - Point Output Model

Böhm-Bawerk was interested to explain why there is a positive rate of interest. One of the special and particularly important reasons for a positive rate of interest which he gave was his law that labour productivity increases with an increasing round-aboutness of production. The degree of round·aboutness is measured by the average period of production. Since the average period of production is a difficult concept we shall now analyse a model in which there can be no doubt about what is meant by the (average) period of production. This is the point input - point output model. We assume that all labour inputs of a process of production are concentrated in one period and that the same is true of outputs. Entrepreneurs have the choice between different production processes which differ in the time distance between labour input and final output and in the productivity ratio (final output per unit of labour input).

On the following diagram we draw a line showing the maximum obtainable productivity ratio q as a function of the period of production T.

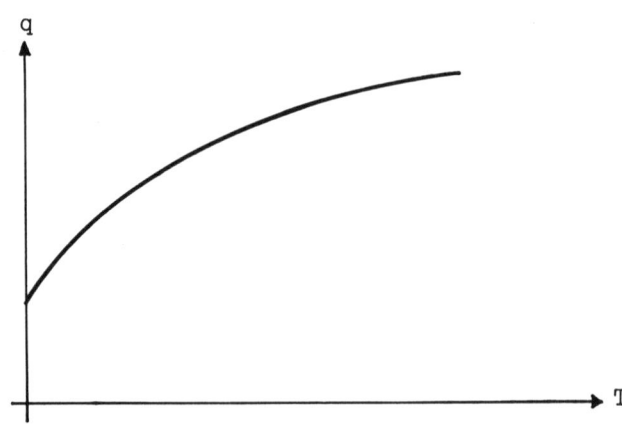

Böhm-Bawerk assumes that this function q(T) is monotonically increasing. But this is at the moment not a necessary assumption. It is plausible at least for a certain range of values of T. Which period of production will be selected by entrepreneurs? For a given real wage rate w (in terms of the final output) a given interest rate r and a given period of production T the costs of employing one worker and compounding the wage paid until the final output accrues is given by

$$w\, e^{rT}.$$

In equilibrium there cannot exist a process which provides an extra profit (in excess of the normal profit on capital) and hence we have for each T the inequality

$$q(T) \leq w\, e^{rT} \quad \text{or} \quad e^{-rT} q(T) \leq w$$

On the other hand at least one process of production must exist which is able to cover it's costs. Thus

$$q(T) = w\, e^{rT} \quad \text{or} \quad e^{-rT} q(T) = w$$

for some T. This is then the value of T which is selected by the entrepreneurs.

We now show that there is an inverse relation between the rate of interest and the chosen period of production. Let T_0 be the period of production chosen at interest rate r_0 and wage rate w_0, let T_1 be the period of production chosen at interest rate r_1 and wage rate w_1. Let $r_1 > r_0$. We then have

$$e^{-r_0 T_0} q(T_0) = w_0 \geq e^{-r_0 T_1} q(T_1)$$

$$e^{-r_1 T_1} q(T_1) = w_1 \geq e^{-r_1 T_0} q(T_0)$$

Upon multiplying the two left hand sides and the two right hand sides we obtain

$$e^{-(r_0 T_0 + r_1 T_1)} q(T_0) q(T_1) \geq e^{-(r_0 T_1 + r_1 T_0)} q(T_0) q(T_1)$$

or

$$r_0 T_0 + r_1 T_1 \leq r_0 T_1 + r_1 T_0$$

or

$$r_0 (T_0 - T_1) \leq r_1 (T_0 - T_1)$$

Since r_1 is greater than r_0 this implies that $T_0 - T_1$ cannot be negative which was to be shown. Thus the lower the interest rate the more roundabout are the methods of production. An economy with a given "subsistence fund" cannot afford an arbitrarily large period of production because it would be in danger to run out of consumption goods before the processes which are under way provide new consumption goods. It is then the function of the rate of interest to induce producers to choose an appropriate degree of roundaboutness in their production methods.

If the "production function" $q(T)$ is differentiable then the following holds. Since the expression

$$q(T) - e^{+rT} w$$

is maximized at the optimal point T for given r and w we have at this point

$$\frac{dq}{dT} - r e^{rT} w = 0$$

and it follows

$$\frac{dq}{dT} - r q(T) = 0 \quad \text{or} \quad \frac{1}{q(T)} \frac{dq}{dT} = r$$

That is the logarithmic rate of change of productivity as a function of the period of production is just equal to the rate of interest in the optimal point.

The relation between the wage rate and the rate of interest is given by

$$w = e^{-rT} q(T)$$

where T itself is a function of r. Upon differentiation with respect to r we get

$$\frac{dw}{dr} = \frac{\partial w}{\partial T} \cdot \frac{dT}{dr} + \frac{\partial w}{\partial r}$$

but

$$\frac{\partial w}{\partial T} = -r e^{-rT} q(T) + e^{-rT} \frac{dq}{dT} =$$

$$= -r e^{-rT} q(T) + e^{-rT} r q(T) = 0$$

Hence

$$\frac{dw}{dr} = \frac{\partial w}{\partial r} = -T e^{-rT} q(t) = -T w$$

If we consider the rate of interest as the factor price of capital then we know from part one that the slope of the factor price frontier is given by the ratio of the factor quantities times minus one. So here Tw

would have to represent the capital intensity. It is in a way what Böhm-Bawerk has called the subsistence fund per worker, as we have discussed in the last chapter: that is the wage rate times the period of production. As we shall see later, we can generalize this formula, and hence strengthen the argument that there is some meaning to talk about capital as being the wage fund or fund of subsistence.

The value of capital in the usual sense of the word is something else. It is the sum of the values of the intermediate products. Intermediate products which are due to labour inputs T periods ago now have a value of $L_{t-T} e^{rT} w$ where L_{t-T} is the amount of labour used as input at time t-T. If we assume that labour inputs grow exponentially at the rate g we have for the total value of capital

$$V_t = \int_{-T}^{0} L_{t-T} e^{rT} dT =$$

$$= L_t \int_{-T}^{0} e^{-gT} e^{rT} w \, dT = wL_t \frac{1 - e^{(g-r)T}}{r - g}$$

for $r \neq g$ and $V_t = L_t \int_{-T}^{0} w \, dT = wL_t T$ for $r = g$. Thus the value of capital per worker V_t/L_t coincides with the subsistence fund if and only if r and g are equal.

We shall refer to this model as the point input point output model or the standard period of production model. We shall refer to the model presented in the first chapter as the standard production function model. In both cases the models have been constructed in such a way that certain concepts can be easily applied and yield the correct results. But the two models already are inconsistent with each other. The results derived with respect to the production function do not work in the standard period of production model and vice versa. The definition of capital as a factor of production does not work in the present model and the definition of "time" as a factor of production as developed in the present model cannot easily be applied to the standard production function model. Thus the law of higher productivity of higher roundaboutness fails to hold in the standard production function model.

Chapter 6. The Period of Production in More General Models

It is not surprising to find that the summarizing of a complex structure of production relations by a small number of indices or variables should cause difficulties. Yet such attempts have to be made by economic theorists, if they want to improve their understanding of real economies. The fact that production is a process extending through time makes it reasonable to try to summarize this time dimension in one way or another.

Under the assumption made in this part of the book - the absence of fixed capital - the time structure of the production process can be reduced to a frequency distribution of labour inputs on the time axis. In probability theory we are used to summarize distributions by their moments and this is what we try to do in this chapter. The average period of production is the first moment of this distribution, and just as the expected value of a distribution plays a prominent role in probability theory the average period of production should play a prominent role in capital theory. It now turns out that the Böhm-Bawerkian definition of the period of production causes certain difficulties. We have already seen how Böhm-Bawerk tried to get around some of these difficulties. From the point of view of present day economic theory some of his devices, such as the adoption of the simple interest rule instead of the compound interest rule, are not legitimate. Following Hicks and others we therefore introduce a concept of the period of production which weighs labour inputs according to their present value and thereby shifts weights when the rate of interest changes. This may not be very appealing at the first sight, but it turns out to have important advantages.

It appears to be simpler to work with a continuous time model. So we adopt such a model. To produce a certain final output we need a preceding flow of labour inputs $\{\alpha(T)\}$ where T represents the time distance of the input in question from the output. Strictly speaking such a continuous time distribution cannot in general be derived from an input output model with a finite number of distinct commodities. But we consider it to be an approximation to a discrete time model with very small time units.

At the moment the output becomes available the present value of the labour input used T periods ago is given by

$$w \, e^{rT} \, \alpha(T)$$

Thus total production cost of the output is given by

$$w \int_0^\infty e^{rT} \alpha(T)\, dT$$

If we express the real wage rate in terms of the output in question then the price of the output must be unity. Hence

$$1 = w \int_0^\infty e^{rT} \alpha(T)\, dT$$

or

$$w = \frac{1}{\int_0^\infty e^{rT} \alpha(T)\, dT}$$

Now we define the average period of production to be

$$T = \frac{\int_0^\infty e^{rT} \alpha(T)\, T\, dT}{\int_0^\infty e^{rT} \alpha(T)\, dT}$$

That is the time distance of the various labour inputs from the output is weighted by the present value of these inputs. If we now differentiate w with respect to r we get the following from the condition that the price of the output is unity

$$0 = \frac{dw}{dr} \int_0^\infty e^{rT} \alpha(T)\, dT + w \int_0^\infty T e^{rT} \alpha(T)\, dT$$

or

$$\frac{dw}{dr} = - \frac{w \int_0^\infty T e^{rT} \alpha(T)\, dT}{\int_0^\infty e^{rT} \alpha(T)\, dT} = -wT$$

The slope of the wage interest curve corresponding to a given production technique is given by what we have called the fund of subsistence, if we introduce the new definition of the average period of production. This again places the fund of subsistence at the place where "capital" as a factor of production should stand.

We see that the period of production, as just defined, could be a reasonable indicator of the "capital intensity" of a certain method of production. To make this clearer, we could keep the nominal wage rate constant and see how the costs of production of a final product change in consequence of a change in the interest rate. If the cost price of the output is called p then differentiation of

$$p = \bar{w} \int_0^\infty e^{rT} \alpha(T) \, dT$$

with respect to r yields

$$\frac{\partial p}{\partial r} = \bar{w} \int_0^\infty T e^{rT} \alpha(T) \, dT = T p$$

Then the relative sensitiviy $\frac{1}{p}\frac{\partial p}{\partial r}$ of the production costs with respect to the costs of capital are represented by the average period of production. The relative price of a commodity with respect to another commodity will increase in consequence of rising interest costs, if it's production is more capital intensive that is if it's average period of production is higher than that of the other commodity. In terms of elasticities we get

$$\frac{r}{p} \frac{\partial p}{\partial r} = r T$$

This is to be compared with the usual cost elasticity formula which says

$$\frac{\partial p}{\partial w_1} \cdot \frac{w_1}{p} = \frac{w_1 a_1}{p}$$

where a_1 is the quantity of some input i used per unit of output.

We are of course interested to see how this fund of subsistence is related to the usual value of capital. For this purpose it is convenient to use the national accounting relations

$$c + g v = w + r v$$

where v is the value of capital per worker. The left hand side says that net national product per head is equal to consumption per head plus net investment per head. The right hand side says that net national product per head is equal to the wage rate plus profits per head. Given the technique of production, c is of course independent of the prices and hence we obtain upon differentiation with respect to r

$$g \frac{dv}{dr} = \frac{dw}{dr} + r \frac{dv}{dr} + v$$

If $r = g$ this implies

$$\frac{dw}{dr} = -v$$

Thus at this point we have

$$\frac{dw}{dr} = -v = -wT \quad \text{or} \quad T = \frac{v}{w} = \frac{v}{c}$$

The fund of subsistence and the value of capital are equal if the rate of interest is equal to the rate of growth; also the average period of production is equal to the ratio of capital to the wage bill or the ratio of capital to consumption.

We have proposed to use the concept of "value" of a good as the price which prevails, if the rate of interest is equal to the rate of growth. Thus, if reckoned in "values" the fund of subsistence and the stock of capital coincide. Moreover the period of production, if calculated at the weighting system corresponding to our value definition, had the following intuitively appealing property. We can ask the question: what is the average time distance of todays labour inputs from the final output to which they contribute. We could call this the system's period of production which would be distinguished from the period of production of the single production process which measures the average time distance of it's inputs to it's output. The system's average period of production would then be computed in the following way: If C(t) is the production of consumption goods at time t and if this production is exponentially growing then the number of workers L_T who are engaged in the stage T of the production process at time zero is given by

$$L_T = \alpha(T) C(T) = \alpha(T) e^{gT} C(o)$$

Thus the average time distance of outputs from todays labour inputs is given by

$$T_g = \frac{\int_0^\infty L_T T \, dT}{\int_0^\infty L_T \, dT} = \frac{\int_0^\infty e^{gT} \alpha(T) T \, dT}{\int_0^\infty e^{gT} \alpha(T) dT}$$

which is equal to the period of production if computed with the rate of interest equal to the rate of growth.

We now turn to the case $r \neq g$. We then compute $v = \frac{w - c}{r - g}$

Graphically the value of capital per worker is given by the slope of the line which connects the (c,g)-point and the (w,r)-point on the wage interest or consumption growth curve. Since Tw is the slope of this curve at the (w,r)-point the two variables are related like the marginal change of w to the average change of w as r moves away from g. Thus, if the wage interest curve of a given technique is concave and if the rate of interest is greater than the rate of growth, then wT will be smaller than

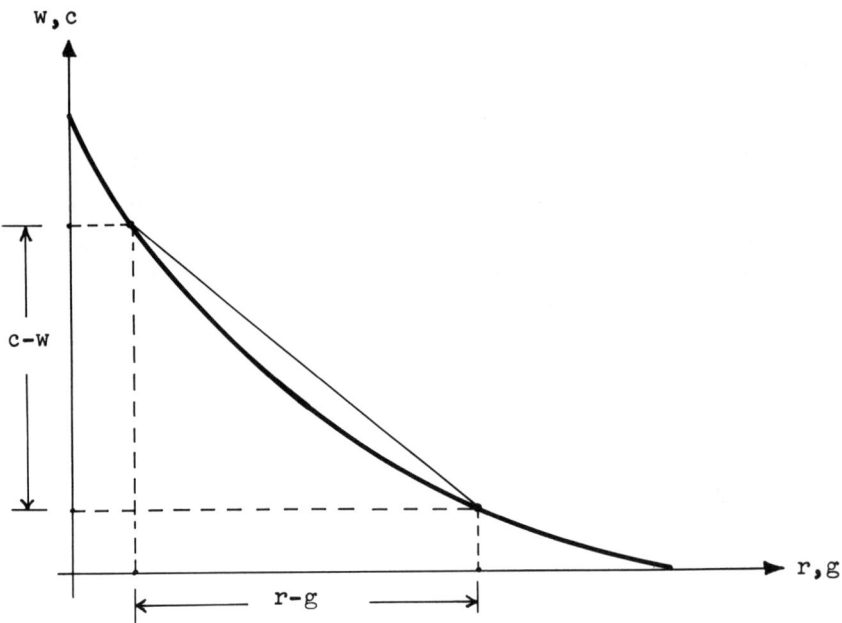

v or T will be smaller than $\frac{v}{w}$. Below we shall prove that T is an increasing function of r. Since a convex wage interest curve implies that v decreases with increasing r we get from cT = v at r = g that cT > v for r > g or T > $\frac{v}{c}$. We thus have an upper and a lower bound for the estimation of T

$$\frac{v}{c} < T < \frac{v}{w}$$

For empirical purposes this allows to get close approximations for the real value of T, given that we can estimate v, c and w.

As for two examples we may take a quick look at the two standard models. The standard production function model has, as we have shown, a linear wage interest curve. This implies that wT = $-\frac{dw}{dr}$ is a constant. Hence T must increase as r increases and therefore w falls. On the other hand in the standard period of production model T is a constant. This implies that w = e^{-rT} q **declines exponentially with increasing r** (we exclude here the substitution of techniques). The value of capital clearly also declines as r increases, since the wage interest curve in this case is convex.

We are now interested better to understand the curvature of the wage interest curve for a given technique of production. For this purpose we differentiate the equation

$$\frac{dw}{dr} = - w T$$

and get

$$\frac{d^2w}{dr^2} = - \frac{dw}{dr} T - w \frac{dT}{dr}$$

Now we have to compute $\frac{dT}{dr}$ from the formula for T

$$\frac{dT}{dr} = \frac{(\int_0^\infty e^{rT} \alpha(T) dT) (\int_0^\infty e^{rT} \alpha(T) T^2 dT)}{(\int_0^\infty e^{rT} \alpha(T) dT)^2} -$$

$$- \frac{(\int_0^\infty e^{rT} \alpha(T) T \, dT) (\int_0^\infty e^{rT} \alpha(T) T dT)}{(\int_0^\infty e^{rT} \alpha(t) dT)^2} =$$

$$= \frac{\int_0^\infty e^{rT} \alpha(T) dT}{\int_0^\infty e^{rT} \alpha(T) dT} - \overline{T}^2 =$$

$$\int_0^\infty \frac{e^{rT} \alpha(T)}{\int_0^\infty e^{rs} \alpha(s) ds} (T^2 - \overline{T}^2) \, dT = \text{Var} \left(\frac{e^{rT} \alpha(T)}{\int_0^\infty e^{rT} \alpha(T) dT} \right)$$

The first derivative of T with respect to r is then given by the variance of the distribution of labour inputs (corrected for present value). The curvature of the wage interest function as expressed by the second derivative is hence

$$\frac{d^2w}{dr^2} = - \frac{dw}{dr} T - w \frac{dT}{dr} = w T^2 - w S^2$$

where S^2 is the variance of the input distribution.

The second derivative is zero everywhere when $S^2 = T^2$ everywhere. This is only the case for the exponential distribution $\alpha(T) = \alpha(o) e^{-\gamma T}$. We thus see that the standard production function model presupposes an **exponential distribution of labour inputs.**

It should be noted that in the circulating capital model all information about the flow of labour inputs is contained in the wage-interest curve. If we know the latter then the flow of labour inputs per unit of output is uniquely determined. To prove this, note that without loss of generality we can assume that the labour input integral

$$\int_0^\infty \alpha(T) \, dT = 1$$

(this is simply a matter of choosing the appropriate unit of measurement for the output). It then can be treated like a probability distribution. By differentiating the expression

$$\frac{1}{w} = \int_0^\infty e^{rT} \alpha(T) dT$$

with respect to r at $r=0$ we obtain

$$\frac{d}{dr}\left(\frac{1}{w}\right)_{r=0} = \int_0^\infty T e^{rT} \alpha(T) dT = \int_0^\infty T \alpha(T) dT = m_1$$

Successive differentiation yields

$$\left(\frac{d^2 \frac{1}{w}}{dr^2}\right)_{r=0} = \int_0^\infty T^2 e^{rT} \alpha(T) dT = \int_0^\infty T^2 \alpha(T) dT = m_2$$

$$\frac{d^k \frac{1}{w}}{dr^k}\bigg|_{r=0} = \int_0^\infty T^k e^{rT} \alpha(T) dT = \int_0^\infty T^k \alpha(T) dT = m_k$$

The k-th derivative with respect to r at $r=0$ is equal to the k-th moment m_k of the distribution. We therefore know: If $w(r)$ is a wage interest curve of a circulating capital technique of production then it is infinitely often differentiable at $r=0$ and the k-th derivative of $\frac{1}{w}$ with respect to r is equal to the k-th moment of the input distribution. But, by assumption there exists $r>0$ that

$$\frac{1}{w}(r) = \int_0^T e^{rT} \alpha(T) dT = \int_0^\infty \sum_{k=0}^\infty \frac{(rT)^k}{k!} \alpha(T) dT = \sum_{k=0}^\infty \int_0^\infty \frac{(rT)^k}{k!} \alpha(T) dT =$$

$\sum_{k=0}^{\infty} \frac{m_k}{k!} r^k$ is finite. But by a theorem in probability theory a distribution is uniquely determinded by it's moments, if there exists $r > 0$ such that $\sum_{k=0}^{\infty} \frac{m_k}{k!} r^k$ is finite (**M.Fisz**, Probability Theory and Mathematical Statistics, 3rd edition, New York 1963, p.73).

This is the proof that the wage interest curve $w(r)$ contains all information about the distribution of original inputs.

Chapter 7. Substitution, Switching of Techniques

In the first part of these lecture notes we considered substitution in the context of more than one original factor of production. We saw how the ratio of the wages of the primary inputs determined the choice of the technique of production. We are now interested to apply an analogous analysis in a context where one of the primary inputs is replaced by "capital" and the corresponding input wage rate is replaced by the rate of interest. We know from the preceding chapters that the wage interest curve for a given technique of production is not necessarily a straight line. Thus the concept of employment intensities of the two inputs labour and capital does not have an unambiguous meaning. The problems for analysis therefore become more complicated.

This should not come as a surprise. After all the correct generalization from part one is to say the following: the introduction of the time dimension into the production process makes it necessary to distinguish between as many different primary factors of production as we distinguish unit periods of time. If we would work in such an infinitely dimensional space every technique of production would be represented by a hyperplane in the wage space that is by the natural generalization of a straight line in the two dimensional space. We could prove nonreswitching theorems etc. From the economic point of view everything would be straightforward. But this is not the interesting question to ask. What we should investigate in capital theory is the possibility of aggregation over these different dated labour inputs in one way or another. What do we gain by mapping this infinitely dimensional space into the two dimensional (r, w)-space?

If different techniques of production are available in the economy then the following diagram shows how a technique is chosen as a function of the rate of interest. Competition on the labour market will bid up the

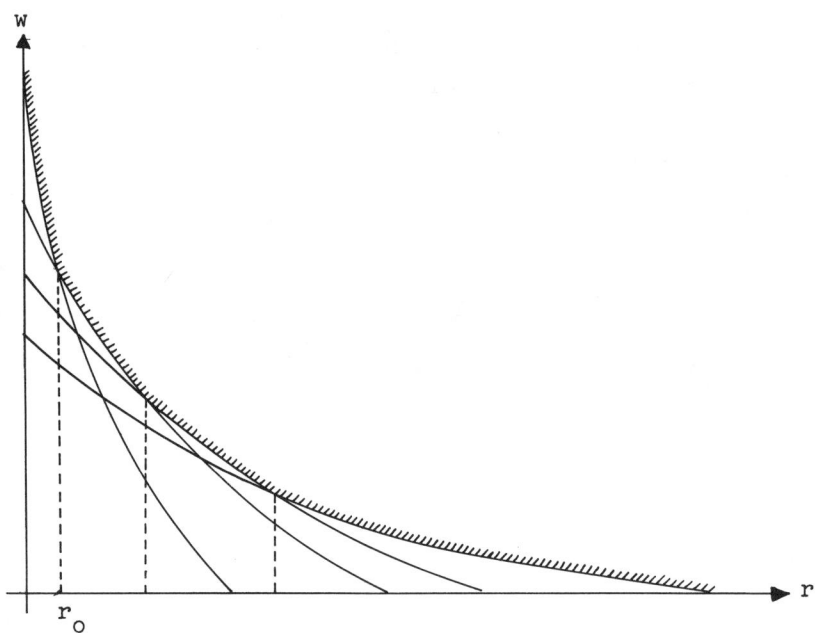

the wage rate until there is only one technique (or in certain special cases two techniques) which can be operated without loss at the prevailing interest rate and wage rate. If the number of different techniques is finite, then a given technique, if it is applied at all, is applied at every interest rate within a given interval. The border points of these intervals on the r-axis are points at which two techniques (or, in exceptional cases, three and more) are equally efficient in the sense that they can operate at the same maximum wage rate. These border points are called switch points. As the rate of interest increases the economy switches at such a point from one technique to another technique.

Consider now such a switch point r_o where the two wage interest curves $w_1(r)$ and $w_2(r)$ intersect so that $w_1(r_o) = w_2(r_o)$. We assume that $w_1(r) > w_2(r)$ for $r < r_o$ and r sufficiently close to r_o and $w_2(r) > w_1(r)$ for $r > r_o$ and r sufficiently close to r_o. This means that as the rate of interest increases the economy switches at point r_o from technique 1 to technique 2. Since we can always differentiate the wage interest curve of a given technique which only uses circulating capital we have

$$\left.\frac{dw_2}{dr}\right|_{r=r_o} > \left.\frac{dw_1}{dr}\right|_{r=r_o}$$ and it thus follows that

$-w_2 T_2 (r_o) > - w_1 T_1 (r_o)$ where T_2 and T_1 are the periods of production of the two techniques. Since $w_1 (r_o) = w_2(r_o)$ we then get

$$- T_2 (r_o) > - T_1 (r_o) \quad \text{or}$$

$$T_2 (r_o) < T_1 (r_o)$$

Thus we obtain the following result. At any given switch point one switches from the technique with the higher period of production to the technique with the lower period of production as the rate of interest increases. We have argued earlier that the period of production is a good measure for the "capital intensity" of a production technique. This last result reenforces this view: any substitution between methods of production is characterized by a tendency towards a reduction of capital intensity as the rate of interest increases.

Our defintion of the period of production is not independent of the rate of interest. We then cannot rule out that at one rate of interest technique 1 and at another rate of interest technique 2 is more capital intensive. This may lead to the following situation (assuming that there are only two techniques available in the economy).

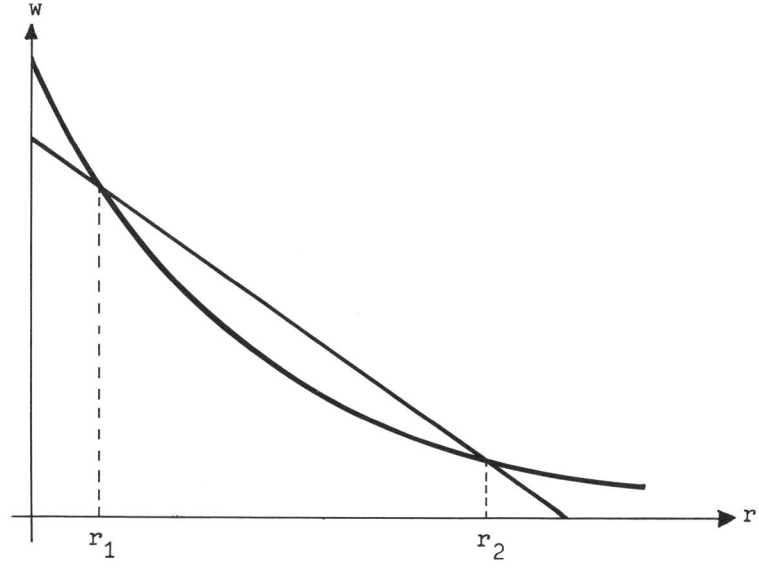

Technique 1 is more efficient than technique 2 at very low and at very high interest rates. In the intermediate range technique 2 is more efficient. There is no general principle which could prevent such a situation.

To fix ideas let us take the following example. Let technique 1 be of the point input - point output type with a given time distance T_1 between input and output. The wage interest curve is then an exponential curve. Let technique 2 be of the standard production function type, which implies a straight line for the wage interest curve. The period of production increases as the rate of interest increases. In fact the time structure of direct and indirect labour inputs is exponential in this case. We have $\alpha(T) = a e^{-\gamma T}$ and thus the period of production T_2 is given by

$$T_2 = \frac{\int_0^\infty e^{-\gamma T} e^{rT} T \, dT}{a \int_0^\infty e^{-\gamma T} e^{rT} dT} = \frac{\frac{1}{(\gamma-\gamma)^2}}{\frac{1}{\gamma-r}} = \frac{1}{\gamma-r}$$

T_2 varies from $\frac{1}{\gamma}$ to infinity as r varies from zero to γ. At $r=\gamma$ the wage rate becomes zero. If now $T_1 > \frac{1}{\gamma}$ then for small interest rates we have $T_1 > T_2$ and then the point input-point output technique is more capital intensive than the standard production function technique. Hence at some point r_1 the latter technique becomes more efficient. But as the rate of interest rises T_2 rises too and hence from a certain rate of interest onwards T_2 is larger than T_1 and we now have to consider technique 2 to be the more capital intensive technique. From a certain rate of interest r_2 onwards the wage rate that can be paid by technique 1 is again higher than with technique 2 which now bears a much higher burden of capital intensity.

It is essential for our argument that one technique has a much higher dispersion of labour inputs than the other technique. It is then necessary to introduce at least the second moment of the labour input distribution and we could try to **replace** the traditional mean-time distance approach by a mean-variance approach. For example the discrepancy between the value of the capital stock per man and the slope of the wage interest curve could be explained in terms of the variance of the labour-input distribution.

The maximum number of switch points can be related to the characterization of the input distribution by it's moments. Assume there are n different switch points between two techniques. Consider two adjacent switch points r_i and r_{i+1} with $r_i < r_{i+1}$. Then $w_1(r_i) = w_2(r_i)$, $w_1(r_{i+1}) = w_2(r_{i+1})$ and let $w_2(r) > w_1(r)$ for $r_i < r < r_{i+1}$. Then clearly $w_2'(r_i) > w_1'(r_i)$ and $w_2'(r_{i+1}) < w_1'(r_{i+1})$ which implies there must be some "switch point" for the derivative, r' such that $r_i < r' < r_{i+1}$ and $w_2'(r') = w_1'(r')$, since $w_1(r)$ and $w_2(r)$ are infinitely differentiable and thus all derivatives are continuous. Thus there are at least $n-1$ "switch points" of second order, that is, points where the derivatives of the wage interest curves are equal. In a similar way we prove that there are at least $n-2$ "switch points" for the second derivatives $w_1''(r)$ and $w_2''(r)$, in general that there are $n-k$ "switch points" for the k-th derivatives of $w_1(r)$ and $w_2(r)$. This implies the following: If for two wage interest curves $w_1(r)$ and $w_2(r)$ the k-th derivative $w_2^{(k)}(r)$ is unambiguously greater than $w_1^{(k)}(r)$ then there are <u>at most</u> k switch points between $w_1(r)$ and $w_2(r)$. Similarly we can derive: If the **k-th derivative** of $\frac{1}{w_1(r)}$ is unambiguously greater than $\frac{1}{w_2(r)}$ then there are at most k switch points between $w_1(r)$ and $w_2(r)$. The k-th derivative of

$$\frac{1}{w(r)} = \int_0^\infty e^{rT} \alpha(T) dT \quad \text{is given by}$$

$$\left(\frac{1}{w(r)}\right)^{(k)} = \int_0^\infty T^k e^{rT} \alpha(T) dT$$

Let $m_k(r)$, the k-th moment of the input cost distribution be given by

$$m_k(r) = \frac{\int_0^\infty T^k e^{rT} \alpha(T) dT}{\int_0^\infty e^{rT} \alpha(T) dT} = w(r) \left(\frac{1}{w(r)}\right)^{(k)}$$

$m_k(r)$ varies of course with the weighting system e^{rT} of the labour inputs. But we may find a k such that k-th moment of $\{\alpha_1(T)\}$ is unambiguously reater than the k-th moment of $\{\alpha_2(T)\}$. We then get the following theorem: If the $m_k^1(r)$ is unambiguously greater than $m_k^2(r)$ then there are at most k switch points between the two techniques. This theorem is a generalization of the theorem that reswitching cannot take place if the period of production of one of the techniques is unambiguously larger than the period of production of the other technique.
<u>Proof of the theorem.</u> Assume the contrary. Then we find $n > k$ switch points. This implies that we can find two switch points such that $\left(\frac{1}{w_1(r)} - \frac{1}{w_2(r)}\right)^{(k)}$ has opposite signs. But then $m_k^1(r) - m_k^2(r)$ has opposite signs at these switch points which contradicts the assumption.

It should be stressed that this is a theorem about the maximum number of switch points. The actual number of switch points between any two techniques may be much lower.

The possibility of the existence of two switch points between two techniques shows that consumption per head (and hence output per head) in a stationary economy is not necessarily a monotonically decreasing function of the rate of interest. In a stationary economy we have the equation

$$c = w(r) + rv$$

Hence for techniques 1 and 2

$$c_1 = w_1(o), \quad c_2 = w_2(o)$$

In the particular case we discussed earlier we have $c_1 > c_2$.

Now $c(r) = c_1$ for $r < r_1$ and $r > r_2$

$$c(r) = c_2 \text{ for } r_1 < r < r_2$$

This implies that $c(r)$ is greater at some value $r > r_2$ than at some value $r < r_2$. Similarly the value of capital does not necessarily decrease as a more "capital intensive" technique is replaced by a less "capital intensive" technique. From the equation above we have for a stationary economy

$$v = \frac{c-w}{r}$$

At the switch point r_2 c increases as we switch to a less capital intensive technique. Hence v increases too and therefore in the neighborhood of r we have the result that the value of the capital goods used at a higher interest rate is higher than the value of the capital goods used at the lower interest rate, even if the capital goods are evaluated at the same prices, namely those prices prevailing at the interest rate r_2.

Chapter 8. The Dynamic Nonsubstitution Theorem. Generalization of the Elasticity of Substitution.

In part I we have proved the nonsubstitution theorem. The proof rested on the uniqueness of the solution of the system of the price equations

$$p = \phi(\bar{w}, p)$$

for any given w, where ϕ was the unit cost function as a function of input prices. In the model where time enters into the production process the unit cost function changes to $\phi(\bar{w}, r, p)$. But otherwise it keeps all relevant properties. For given r ϕ_i remains homogeneous of degree one in $\bar{w}$ and p, and ϕ_i remains a strictly increasing function of $\bar{w}$, if a_{oi} is positive. This is true for all i and thus we can show the uniqueness of the solution of the system of price equations

$$p = \phi(\bar{w}, r, p)$$

for given $\bar{w}$ and r. We thus can prove what sometimes is referred to as the dynamic nonsubstitution theorem: If the rate of interest is given then all relative prices in the system and the optimal technique of production are determined.

This dynamic nonsubstituion theorem tells us that the technique which maximizes the real wage rate for a given interest rate is independent of the standard commodity basket s in terms of which the real wage rate is defined.

I now want to introduce the concept of elasticity of substitution between techniques. The elasticity of substitution usually is defined for linear homogeneous production functions with two inputs. It is a measure of the possibility to substitute one input for the other input when input prices change. Its standard definition is given by the equation

$$\sigma = \frac{w_1 / w_2}{q_1 / q_2} \frac{d(q_1 / q_2)}{d(w_1 / w_2)}$$

where w_1 and w_2 are the input prices and q_1 and q_2 are the input quantities. It is well known that σ can be written in the form

$$\sigma = - \frac{w_1}{a_1} \frac{da_1}{dw_1}$$

where a_1 is the quatity of input 1 per unit of output. In particular, if input 1 is "capital" in the standard production function modell, and if a_1 is the capital output ratio then

$$\sigma = - \frac{r}{a_1} \frac{da_1}{dr} = \left| \frac{r}{a_1} \frac{da_1}{dr} \right|$$

that is the elasticity of substitution is the absolute value of the elasticity of the capital output ratio with respect to the interest rate.

In the more general framework which we consider here we know that it is difficult to use the value of capital per man as a measure of the capital intensity of production. The reason is not so much that even with given techniques of production the value of capital depends on prices, e.g. on the interest rate. This difficulty could be overcome. But the fact that the value of given physical capital goods depends on the rate of interest is only the dual manifestation of the deeper difficulty that the value of the capital goods for a given technique and given prices depends on the rate of growth of the system. Even if we decide about the prices with which to measure the size of the capital stock this measure of the capital stock is not uniquely defined by the methods of production used. It can therefore not serve as an unambiguous indicator for the possibilities of substitution. The period of production as a measure of capital intensity does have the advantage that it is uniquely defined on any point of the wage interest curve and **thus** does not depend on the product mix between consumption and investment goods. It is therefore a better starting point for measuring the substitution possibilities between techniques.

But we have to be careful when we give a precise definition of the elasticity of substitution, since the period of production for a given technique also depends on the rate of interest. We have to distinguish between changes in the period of production due to changes in the weighting system and changes in the period of production due to changes in the techniques of production. We introduce the following notation. Let θ be an index for the techniques of production. A specific technique gets index θ_o, say, if it is the most efficient (wage rate maximizing) technique at the interest rate $r = \theta_o$. We thus parametrize the techniques according to the rate of interest at which the techniques are used. But in order to distinguish the technique parameter from the rate of interest itself we give it the symbol θ. If a technique is used at more than one interest rate then we treat it as if it were a different technique at each different interest rate at which it is used. But this is just a matter of convention since the physical characteristics of the "different" technique are the same in such a case. Our measure for the elasticity of substitution will be zero in such a case. To give a proper definition of the elasticity of substitution in terms of derivatives we have to assume that all magnitudes involved are differentiable functions of θ. This assumption is not satisfied if there are only a finite number of switch points. But under analogous conditions the ordinary concept also breaks down. Generalizations for the discrete case are easily developed. They are less elegant, though.

We then consider T, the period of production, as a function of the parameter for the weighting system of the time flow of inputs, r, and as a function of the parameter of the technique in use, θ. For a given θ we already know that $T(\theta, r)$ has the following partial derivative with respect to r

$$T_2(\theta, r) = \frac{\partial T(\theta, r)}{\partial r} = S^2(\theta, r)$$

where S^2 is the variance of the time flow of inputs. A change in the relative capital intensity which is not just a consequence of a change in the weighting system is reflected in

$$T_1(\theta, r) = \frac{\partial T(\theta, r)}{\partial \theta}$$

We already have shown that $T_1(\theta, r)$ will always be nonpositive. One way to define the elasticity of substitution might therefore be

$$- T_1(\theta, r) \frac{\theta}{T}$$

But this concept of elasticity of substitution is not yet optimal. Firstly, it does not agree with the usual definition in the special case of the standard production function model. But secondly it reflects too a superficial view of the changes in the cost of capital which bring about the substitution.

We have shown earlier that the elasticity of total production cost of a commodity with respect to the rate of interest is given by rT. This was compared with $w_i a_i/p$ the elasticity of total cost with respect to price changes for some input i. This latter elasticity is equal to the share of input i in total costs. We now can interpret the usual elasticity of substitution to be an indicator of the ability of the production system to compensate input price developments in their impact on the relative cost weight of the input, by changes in the input quantities. If the elasticity of substitution is less than one this compensation is not completely succesful. If the elasticity of substitution is equal to one the input output coefficient is proportinal to the inverse of the input price (in terms of the output) and thus $w_i a_i/p$ is a constant. If the elasticity of substitution is greater than one we have overcompensation of price changes by quantity changes and $w_i a_i/p$ is a decreasing function of w_i.

In our more general model we represent the relative importance of capital for the production process by the expression $rT(\theta r)$. This is an expression which is well defined whenever r and θ are determined, just as $\frac{w_i a_i}{p}$ is well defined whenever w_i and the method of production in the conventional model are determined. We therefore define the elasticity of substitution to be the percentage change of rT due to a change in the technique of production which is elicited by a one percent change of rT due to a change in prices (here it is a change in the rate of interest). This means

$$\sigma = - \frac{1}{rT(\theta,r)} \frac{\partial (rT(r,\theta))}{\partial \theta} \Big/ \frac{1}{rT(\theta,r)} \frac{\partial (rT(r,\theta))}{\partial r}$$

evaluated at the point $\theta = r$. The numerator of this expression shows the percentage change of rT, when the technique parameter changes by one unit (as a consequence of a change in the interest rate by the same amount, since in equilibrium we always have $\theta = r$). The denominator shows the corresponding change of rT, when the price parameter changes by one unit. The elasticity of substitution is then

$$\sigma = \frac{-r \frac{\partial (T(r,\theta))}{\partial \theta}}{T + r \frac{\partial T(r,\theta)}{\partial r}} = \frac{-\frac{r}{T} \frac{\partial T(r,\theta)}{\partial \theta}}{1 + \frac{r}{T} \frac{\partial T(r,\theta)}{\partial r}}$$

This definition yields the results which we want in several special cases. For example it is a generalization of the usual definition of elasticity of substitution. To prove this we apply the formula to the standard production function model. Here we have the equation

$$q = f(v)$$

where q is net output per worker and v is the capital intensity. We furthermore have

$$r = f'(v)$$
$$w = f(v) - v f'(v)$$

The capital output ratio is then $\beta = \frac{v}{f(v)}$ and hence the elasticity of substitution in the conventional sense is

$$\sigma = -\frac{r}{\beta} \frac{d\beta}{dr} = -\left(\frac{r}{v} \frac{dv}{dr} - \frac{r}{f(v)} \frac{df(v)}{dr} \right) =$$

$$= -\frac{r}{v} \frac{dv}{dr} \left(1 - \frac{v}{f(v)} \frac{df(v)}{dv} \right) =$$

$$= -\frac{r}{v} \frac{dv}{dr} \left(1 - \frac{rv}{f(v)} \right) = -\frac{r}{v} \frac{dv}{dr} \frac{w}{f(v)}$$

On the other hand our new definition of the elasticity of substitution in this case implies the following

$$T = -\frac{1}{w} \frac{dw}{dr} = \frac{1}{w} v$$

Now v is constant as long as θ is constant and for w we have

$$\left. \frac{\partial w}{\partial \theta} \right|_{\theta=r} = 0$$

since w is maximized with respect to θ at $\theta=r$, given r. So we get $\frac{\partial w}{\partial r} = \frac{dw}{dr}$ and

$$\frac{\partial T}{\partial r} = \frac{\partial T}{\partial w} \cdot \frac{\partial w}{\partial r} = -\frac{v}{w^2} \frac{\partial w}{\partial r} = \frac{v^2}{w^2} = T^2$$

$$\frac{r}{T} \frac{\partial T}{\partial r} = \frac{r}{T} T^2 = rT = r \frac{v}{w}$$

and

$$\frac{\partial T}{\partial \theta} = \frac{1}{w} \frac{dv}{dr}$$

$$\frac{r}{T} \frac{\partial T}{\partial \theta} = \frac{r}{v} \frac{dv}{dr} \quad \text{from which follows}$$

$$\sigma = \frac{\frac{r}{v} \frac{dv}{dr}}{1+\frac{rv}{w}} = \frac{\frac{r}{v} \frac{dv}{dr}}{\frac{f(v)}{w}} = -\frac{r}{v} \frac{dv}{dr} \frac{w}{f(v)}$$

Thus the two definitions give the same result and the new definition can be considered to be a true generalization of the old definition.

The next example is concerned with an economy in which the relative shares of capital and labour are independent of the rate of interest. It is a generalization of the Cobb-Douglas case in the standard production function model. For a fixed $\bar{\theta}$ let the wage interest curve be given by

$$w = f(r, \bar{\theta})$$

Now assume that there exists a class of wage interest curves corresponding to a class of production techniques such that

$$f(\theta, \theta) = \left(\frac{\bar{\theta}}{\theta}\right)^\gamma f(\bar{\theta}, \bar{\theta}), \gamma > 0$$

where by $f(\theta, \theta)$ we mean $f(r, \theta)$ with $r = \theta$, and

$$f(r, \theta) = f(\theta, \theta) \frac{f(r\frac{\bar{\theta}}{\theta}, \bar{\theta})}{f(\bar{\theta}, \bar{\theta})} = \left(\frac{\theta}{\bar{\theta}}\right)^\gamma f(r\frac{\bar{\theta}}{\theta}, \bar{\theta})$$

This implies that the different wage interest curves have similar shape. They are different only in their slope and thus for different interest rates different techniques maximize the wage rate. If we assume that $f(r, \theta)$ is maximized at the point $\theta = r$ with respect to θ then the envelope of all curves $f(r, \theta)$ and hence the economy's wage interest curve is given by

$$w(r) = f(r, r) = \bar{\theta}^\gamma f(\bar{\theta}, \bar{\theta}) r^{-\gamma}$$

In a stationary economy we obtain the following formula for the distribution of income. The value of the capital stock is given by

$$v = \frac{c - w}{r} = \frac{f(0, \theta) - f(r, \theta)}{r} \quad \text{for } \theta = r, \text{ hence}$$

$$v = \left(\frac{\bar{\theta}}{r}\right)^{\gamma} \frac{f(0,\bar{\theta}) - f(\bar{\theta},\bar{\theta})}{r}$$

$$\frac{rv}{w} = \frac{\left(\frac{\bar{\theta}}{r}\right)^{\gamma}(f(0,\bar{\theta}) - f(\bar{\theta},\bar{\theta}))}{\frac{\bar{\theta}}{r}^{\gamma} f(\bar{\theta},\bar{\theta})} = \frac{f(0,\bar{\theta}) - f(\bar{\theta},\bar{\theta})}{f(\bar{\theta},\bar{\theta})}$$

Here the distribution of income is independent of the rate of interest. In this special model we have for $\theta = r$

$$T(r,\theta) = -\frac{1}{w}\frac{dw}{dr} = \frac{\gamma \bar{\theta}^{\gamma} f(\bar{\theta},\bar{\theta}) r^{-(1+\gamma)}}{\bar{\theta}^{\gamma} f(\bar{\theta},\bar{\theta}) r^{-\gamma}} = \frac{\gamma}{r}$$

This implies that

$$\frac{r}{T}\frac{dT}{dr} = \frac{r}{T}\left(\frac{\partial T}{\partial \theta} + \frac{\partial T}{\partial r}\right) = -1$$

or, since $\theta = r$

$$\frac{\theta}{T}\frac{\partial T}{\partial \theta} = -\left(1 + \frac{r}{T}\frac{\partial T}{\partial r}\right)$$

and hence

$$\sigma = -\frac{\frac{\theta}{T}\frac{\partial T}{\partial \theta}}{1 + \frac{r}{T}\frac{\partial T}{\partial r}} = 1$$

It should be noted that the distribution of income is no longer in general independent of the rate of interest, if the rate of growth is not equal to zero. The income distribution is in general then determined by $\frac{g}{r}$. But it can be shown that it is not possible to find a class of wage interest curves such that the relative income distribution is independent of the rate of interest at all rates of growth unless the single members of the class of wage interest curves has the property that the income distribtuion is independent of the growth rate. This latter property implies that the wage interest curves are straight lines which is only the case in the standard production function model.

The third example which I want to discuss is the point input - point output model. Here T is fixed whenever θ is fixed and thus the elasticity of substitution can be written as

$$\sigma = -\frac{\theta}{T}\frac{\partial T}{\partial \theta} \quad \text{or}$$

simply
$$\sigma = -\frac{rdT}{Tdr}$$

The wage rate and output per man $q(T)$ are related by the formula
$$w(T) = e^{-rT} q(T)$$
and thus the share of wages $\frac{w}{q}$ depends on the rate of interest in the following fashion
$$\frac{1}{\frac{w}{q}} \frac{d\frac{w}{q}}{dr} = \frac{d \log \frac{w}{q}}{dr} = -\frac{drT}{dr} = -1 + \sigma$$

In particular if the elasticity of substitution is a constant we obtain for $\sigma = 1$
$$q(T) = A T^n, \quad r = \frac{n}{T}, \quad w = e^{-rT} q(T) = q(T) = q(T)e^{-n}$$
$$n > 0$$

which implies constant relative shares. For $\sigma \neq 1$, but constant, we get for $\alpha = \frac{1}{\sigma}$
$$q(T) = A e^{\frac{\beta}{1-\alpha} T^{1-\alpha}} \qquad r = \beta T^{-\alpha}$$
$$\frac{w(T)}{q(T)} = e^{-rT} = e^{-\beta T^{1-\alpha}}$$

This is very similar to the usual CES function. For $\sigma < 1$ and hence $\alpha > 1$ we see that $q(T)$ is bounded above: the share of wages approaches one as the methods of production become more capital intensive. For $\sigma > 1$ we have $q(T)$ as an unbounded function and the share of wages approaches zero as T becomes large.

Chapter 9. Wicksell Effect. Marginal Productivity of Capital

In general relative prices of commodities change as the rate of interest changes. This is only not the case in the standard production function model where there is basically only one commodity and therefore there exists no problem of relative prices of produced commodities. The fact that the value of a given physical capital stock depends on the rate of interest (via the prices of the capital goods) is known as the Wicksell effect. Wicksell was the first to study it systematically. It is this Wicksell effect which makes it difficult to treat "capital" as a factor of production like any other homogeneous factor of production.

The size of the Wicksell effect can be computed from the wage interest curve for a given technique of production. By the dual interpretation of the wage interest curve as the consumption growth curve we know that for $r - g \neq 0$

$$v = \frac{c - w}{r - g} = \frac{f(g) - f(r)}{r - g}$$

holds, where f is the wage interest curve. By differentiating v with respect to r we obtain

$$\frac{dv}{dr} = \frac{-(r-g) f'(r) - (f(g)-f(v))}{(r-g)^2} =$$

$$= \frac{1}{r-g} \left(T(r) \, w \, (r) - v \right)$$

The Wicksell effect is thus proportional to the difference between the fund of subsistence Tw and the value of the capital stock.

There exists a dual of the Wicksell effect: the change in the value of capital due to a change in the rate of growth of the system. It is

$$\frac{dv}{dg} = \frac{(r-g) f'(g) + (f(r) - f(r))}{(r-g)^2} =$$

$$= \frac{1}{r-g} \left(v - T(g) \, c \, (g) \right)$$

The change in the value of the capital stock per man as a consequence of a change in the rate of growth indicates that the distribution of income is not independent of the rate of growth. But this is just a special case of the fact that at a given rate of interest the income distribution depends on the composition of final demand whenever the capital intensity of production varies from commodity to commodity.

We now turn to the question whether the concept of marginal productivity of capital has any clear meaning. For this purpose we have to consider an economy with possibilities of substitution. We parametrize the techniques again by θ, the rate of interest at which they are used. For the purpose of the following argument it is useful to write the value of the capital stock as the product of a quantity vector and a price vector $v = p \cdot z$.

Now for a given rate of growth the quantity vector depends only on the technique θ whereas the price vector depends on the rate of interest and the technique in use. But, if for any r the most efficient technique (which is $\theta = r$) is used then we can think of p just as a function of r. The nonsubstitution theorem grants that p is uniquely determined by r. We therefore can write $v = p(r) \cdot z(\theta)$

In equilibrium the prices are such that it is not possible to make profits in production in excess of the normal interest return on capital. This implies that at given equilibrium prices r, $w(r)$, $p(r)$ for all θ the value of net national product is not greater than the income of the factors of production. Thus for every θ we have

$$C(\theta) + g\, p(r)\, z(\theta) \leq w(r) + r\, p(r)\, z(\theta)$$

which we also can write

$$C(\theta) + (g - r)\, p(r)\, z(\theta) - w(r) \leq 0$$

For $\theta = r$ we have the equation

$$C(\theta) + (g - r)\, p(r)\, z(\theta) - w(r) = 0$$

$\theta = r$ then maximizes the left hand expression with respect to θ. If the function of θ can be differentiated with respect to θ we therefore obtain at $\theta = r$

$$\frac{dc}{d\theta} + (g - r)\, p(r)\, \frac{dz}{d\theta} = 0$$

or

$$\frac{dc}{d\theta} + g\, p(r)\, \frac{dz}{d\theta} = r\, p(r)\, \frac{dz}{d\theta}$$

The left hand side is the marginal change in the value of net national product at constant prices as we change θ. The right hand side is the rate of interest times the marginal change in the value of the capital stock. We then obtain the result that, if measured in constant prices, the marginal productivity of capital is equal to the rate of interest. Moreover there exists a (local) law of diminishing marginal returns to capital: If we can differentiate again we get

$$\frac{d^2c}{d\theta^2} + g\, p(r)\, \frac{d^2z}{d\theta^2} \leq r\, p(r)\, \frac{d^2z}{d\theta^2}$$

The rate of change of net national product declines more rapidly than r times the rate of change of capital. Moreover the inequality from which these relations were derived is analogous to a weak global law of decreasing marginal returns to capital. If we put $\theta^* = r$ we have

$$y(r,\theta) - y(r,\theta^*) = C(\theta) - C(\theta^*) + g\, p(r)\, (z(\theta) - z(\theta^*))$$

$$\leq r\, p(r)\, (z(\theta) - z(\theta^*)) = r\, (v(r,\theta) - v(r,\theta^*))$$

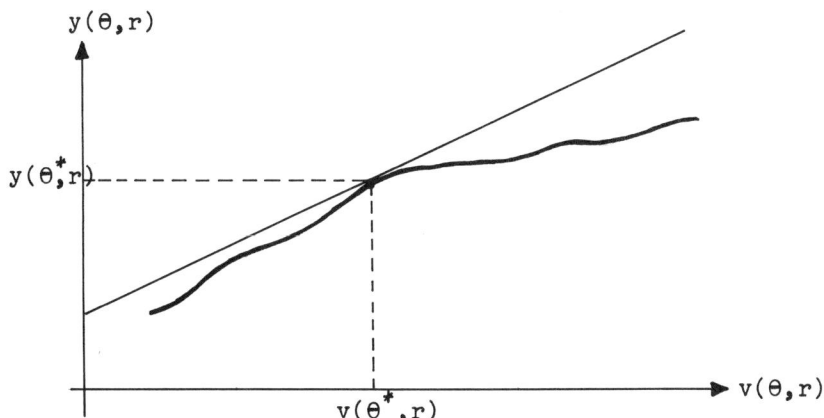

We can extend this result on the marginal productivity interpretation of the rate of interest to the case when $c(\theta)$ and $z(\theta)$ are not differentiable with respect to θ. This is the case of a finite number of techniques. Let us consider a switch point between technique 1 and technique 2. We then have at this switch point

$$c_1 - w_1(r) = (r-g) p^1(r) z^1$$
$$c_2 - w_2(r) = (r-g) p^2(r) z^2$$

Because of the switch point property we have $w_1(r) = w_2(r)$ and because of the nonsubstitution theorem we have $p^1(r) = p^2(r) = p(r)$

Therefore

$$c_1 + g p(r) z^1 = w(r) + r p(r) z^1$$
$$c_2 + g p(r) z^2 = w(r) + r p(r) z^2$$

or

$$(c_2 + g p(r) z^2) - (c_1 + g p(r) z^1) =$$
$$r p(r) (z^2 - z^1)$$

The difference in net product associated with the two techniques can be explained in terms of the difference in the value of capital and the rate of interest in the economy. Thus the marginal productivity interpretation of the rate of interest carries over to the case of a finite number of techniques.

This marginal productivity result is the static counterpart to the well known theorems of Solow about the equivalence of the rate of interest and the marginal social rate of return on savings. Indeed this is easily established. Consider any dynamic path on which the techniques which are competitive at the switch point in question are both used. Assume that the prices remain the same from period to period and are equal to the steady state prices p. Then in each period we have

$$y(t) = c(t) + p \left(z(t+1) - z(t) \right) = w + r p z(t)$$

We can multiply this equation with the labour supply $L(t)$.
We can compare total consumption $\bar{C}(t) = L(t) c(t)$ with total consumption on any other path with the same property of constant prices $\bar{C}'(t) = L(t) c'(t)$ obeying the equation

$$y'(t) = c'(t) + p \left(z'(t+1) - z'(t) \right) = w + r p z'(t)$$

starting from the same initial capital stock $z'(o) = z(o)$ and having the same labour supply. The difference in total consumption $\Delta C(t)$ is then

$$\Delta C(t) = \bar{C}'(t) - \bar{C}(t) = L(t) \left(c'(t) - c(t) \right) =$$
$$= L(t) p \left(- z'(t+1) + z'(t) + r z'(t) + z(t+1) z(t) - r z(t) \right)$$

We then obtain

$$\sum_{t=o}^{\infty} \Delta C(t) \frac{1}{(1+r)^{t+1}} = p \sum_{t=o}^{\infty} \left(z(t+1) - z'(t+1) \right) \frac{L(t)}{(1+r)^{t+1}}$$
$$+ p \sum_{t=o}^{\infty} \left(z'(t) - z(t) \right) \frac{1+r}{(1+r)^{t+1}} L(t) = p \left(z'(o) - z(o) \right)$$

if we assume that

$$\lim_{t \to \infty} \frac{z(t)L(t)}{(1+r)^{t+1}} = \lim_{t \to \infty} \frac{z'(t)L(t)}{(1+r)^{t+1}} = 0.$$

The present value of differences in consumption streams is equal to the difference in the value of capital stocks which implies: the internal social rate of return on savings is equal to the rate of interest.
The only problem which may arise in such dynamic path is that due to non-proportionalities of certain specific inputs there may exist excess capacities of certain inputs with the consequence that their price is zero for certain periods, which violates the condition that the steady state prices prevail. This basically means that the synchronization of production does not work as well on nonsteady state paths, or to put it differently that the production possibility set of consumption goods has a corner point at the steady state path under consideration. Then the social marginal rate of return on savings would not be defined. It still would be true that the right hand side and the left hand side social rate of return on savings are separated from each other by the rate of

interest. This contrasts with a negative result on the average period of production. Böhm-Bawerk showed for his model that an addition of one small unit to the prevailing period of production would raise the product per man by the factor 1+r. This result does not hold here. We only have to refer to the reswitching case in which it happens that a rise in the rate of interest can cause a rise in net national product while it is associated with a fall in the average period of production (for a constant weighting system).

We then obtain, what one could call a dual concept of capital. There is the value of capital per worker and there is the average period of production. Both these concepts are aggregates and in both cases the method of aggregation depends on the rate of interest prevailing in the economy. Each of the two aggregates is not a full substitute for the interpretation of capital as a physical input such as labour or land; but it seems that if they are used together as quantities representing the quantity of capital we can get quite far. Let us recapitulate some of the results which we have obtained.

1. <u>Distribution:</u> The value concept of capital gives us the relative shares of capital and labour in national income for any given combination of r and w. On the other hand the period of production concept of capital gives us the slope of the wage interest curve just as the relative intensity of two inputs gives us the slope of any factor price frontier.

2. <u>Substitution and Marginal Productivity.</u> A rise in the rate of interest may have any effect on the value of capital. But any substitution of techniques caused by a rising rate of interest will have a tendency to diminish the period of production. On the other hand a change in the period of production due to substitution of techniques may have any effect on net national products and may violate Böhm-Bawerks law of a positive marginal productivity of roundaboutness, but the value of capital, if measured in prices corresponding to some interest rate r has a marginal productivity which at the point $\bar{r}$ on the r-axis is equal to the rate of interest.

At last we want to derive what is known as the Golden Rule of Accumulation. The Golden Rule is the solution of the symmetric problem to the wage maximizing problem for a given rate of interest, if we use the dual variables. By the market mechanism the technique θ is selected which maximizes the wage rate. We then have

$$w(r) = \max_{\theta} w(\theta, r)$$

Now we know that the function $c(\theta, g)$ has the same mathematical form as $w(\theta, r)$ and therefore we find

$$\max_{\theta} c(\theta,g) = \max w(\theta,g) = w(g)$$

In words: the technique which maximizes consumption per head for a given rate of growth is the technique which would be selected by the market machanism if the rate of interest were equal to the rate of growth.

This is the Golden Rule of Accumulation.

As was indicated earlier it would not be appropiate to call the Golden Rule path the optimal path if we are interested in a dynamic theory of optimal growth. For such a theory which is not the subject of these lecture notes, we would have to investigate dynamic growth paths in their relation to the objective function of the society. There the Golden Rule path can only serve as a reference path with which the optimal path could be compared.

Part III Fixed Capital

Chapter 1. Machines

We have discussed the classical problems of capital theory by means of a model in which only circulating capital existed. This was consistent with the spirit of classical, Marxian and Austrian capital theory. All these schools were aware of the fact that capital to a large extent consisted of buildings, machines etc. which they called fixed capital. But their theoretical line of thought emphasized that the labour inputs are required before the final outputs become available, an idea which unambiguously is only true for models in which only circulating capital exists. It is the distinctive feature of fixed capital like machines that they are used together with labour inputs over a stretch of time. This has the consequence that final outputs become available before certain labour inputs associated with this same machine are required. We therefore have to consider the complications caused by the partial reversal of the time sequence of labour inputs and final outputs.

Whenever a machine or a building or another piece of fixed capital is used in the production process we have to deal with a production process involving joint products. We can no longer separate completely the production process leading to the production of final outputs in period 1 and the production process producing final outputs in another period, if the same machine is used in these two production process. Final outputs of different periods therefore become joint products.

As an example let us assume that b machines and a units of labour together produce either one new machine or one unit of a consumption good. Moreover, after a machine has been used for one period it depreciates and now represents the fraction γ of one new machine.

Let us assume that we want to produce one unit of the consumption good available at time zero. This inplies that b machines have to be available at time -1. Then at time zero γb machines are still available. They can be used to produce γ comsumption goods at time 1. At time one $\gamma^2 b$ machines are available. They can produce γ^2 consumption goods at time two and so on. We thus get a geometric series of consumption good outputs. If we date again the labour inputs at the time they get paid we have a symmetric geometric time series of labour inputs a, γa, $\gamma^2 a$, $\gamma^3 a$ etc.

If we would look at these outputs and labour inputs only, we would not be able to maintain that labour inputs on average have to be made available earlier than outputs become availabe. But this is of course not the whole story. The b machines available at time -1 had to be constructed earlier. If you want to have b machines at time -1 how many machines do you need at time -2? x machines at time -2 can produce $\frac{x}{b}$ new machines. In addition of these x machines γx are still there at time -1. We thus get the equation

$$b = \frac{x}{b} + \gamma x = x \left(\frac{1}{b} + \gamma \right)$$

or

$$x = b \frac{1}{\frac{1}{b} + \gamma} = b \frac{b}{1 + \gamma b}$$

In a similar way we show that the number of machines at time -3 has to be

$$b \left(\frac{b}{1+\gamma b} \right)^2$$

and so on. We assume that $\frac{b}{1+\gamma b} < 1$, which means that machines are sufficiently productive to be able to overcompensate depreciation by the production of new machines. The labour inputs required to operate the machines are then given by

$$a \left(\frac{b}{1+\gamma b} \right)^{-t}$$

for $t = -1, -2, \ldots$

This is again a geometric series. We thus can describe the production process in terms of final outputs and labour inputs as follows

$$c_t = 0, \quad t = -1, -2, \ldots$$
$$c_t = \gamma^t, \quad t = 0, 1, 2, \ldots$$
$$\alpha_t = a \left(\frac{b}{1+\gamma b} \right)^{-t}, \quad t = -1, -2, \ldots$$
$$\alpha_t = a_\gamma^{\ t}, \quad t = 0, 1, 2, \ldots$$

Although there is a certain amount of overlap of inputs and outputs on the time axis it still is reasonable to think of the labour inputs occurring earlier on average than the final outputs.

To make this precise we can proceed as follows. For reasons of a simpler exposition we again switch to the continuous time case. A given flow of labour inputs α_T and consumption good outputs c_T can be identified with an average period of production for a given interest rate by first computing "the expected value" or "point of gravity" of the labour inputs on the time axis which we call

$$T_\alpha = \frac{\int_{-\infty}^{+\infty} e^{-rT} \alpha_T T \, dT}{\int_{-\infty}^{+\infty} e^{-rT} \alpha_T \, dT}$$

In a similar way we define the point of gravity of the outputs by

$$T_c = \frac{\int_{-\infty}^{+\infty} e^{-rT} c_T T dT}{\int_{-\infty}^{+\infty} e^{-rT} c_T dT}$$

The average period of production is then defined by

$$T = T_c - T_\alpha$$

As in the model of circulating capital we can establish a relationship between the wage interest curve and the period of production. The relation between the wage rate and the interest rate is determined by the no profit - no loss condition which implies

$$\int_{-\infty}^{+\infty} c_T e^{-rT} dT - w \int_{-\infty}^{+\infty} \alpha_T e^{-rT} dT = 0$$

For any given r this is an equation for w. Differentiation with respect to r yields

$$-\int_{-\infty}^{+\infty} c_T e^{-rT} T dT + w \int_{-\infty}^{+\infty} \alpha_T e^{-rT} T dT - \frac{dw}{dr}\int_{-\infty}^{+\infty} \alpha_T e^{-rT} dT = 0$$

or using the equation for w

$$-\frac{\int_{-\infty}^{+\infty} c_T e^{-rT} T dT}{\int_{-\infty}^{+\infty} c_T e^{-rT} dT} + \frac{\int_{-\infty}^{+\infty} \alpha_T e^{-rT} T dT}{\int_{-\infty}^{+\infty} \alpha_T e^{-rT} dT} - \frac{1}{w}\frac{dw}{dr} = 0$$

which can be written as

$$\frac{1}{w}\frac{dw}{dr} = -T_c + T_\alpha = -T$$

Thus this relation generalizes to the case of fixed capital.

In the model of circulating capital we had found a one to one relationship between the structure of the flow of labour inputs per unit of final output and the wage interest curve. And any flow of labour inputs and consumption good outputs which was consistent with the wage interest curve of a technique could be generated by this technique. In this sense the wage interest curve contained all technological information of this technique. This is clearly no longer the case in a model of fixed capital. To see this we only have to look at our simple model discussed above. The wage interest curve, as can easily be seen is given by

$$w = \frac{1 - b(1 - \gamma + r)}{a}$$

This wage interest curve could also be generated by the simple circulating capital model which we discussed at the beginning of part II. We only have to put the labour input coefficient in that model to be equal to $\frac{a}{1+\gamma b}$ and the input output ratio of the commodity itself to be equal to $\frac{b}{1+\gamma b}$.

But clearly by using the simple circulating capital model we can produce a flow of labour inputs and consumption good outputs which cannot be produced by the corresponding fixed capital model. The latter is restricted to flows of consumption good outputs which do not decline by a rate greater than $1-\gamma$ per period. Otherwise some of the machines would be underutilized which means that the wage interest curve could not be supported by the system. Thus the wage interest curve does not give us complete information about the constraints under which we can generate labour input consumption good output paths.

The constraints not reflected in the wage interest curve are not relevant for steady states with which we are mainly concerned in these lecture notes. From any feasible labour consumption path whose integrals converge we can construct an exponentially growing economy in the following way. The production process characterized by these two paths of inputs and outputs has a certain point $T = 0$. This point can be arbitrarily chosen, but once it is chosen we have to keep it fixed. If the production process would not extend into the infinite past we could give the starting point the index $T = 0$. If, as in the circulating capital model is the case, the production process does not extend into the infinite future we could give the end point the index $T = 0$. Otherwise we arbitrarily have to identify some stage of the production process with $T=0$. After that is done we can date a specific production process in calender time by determining at which moment t it reaches stage $T = 0$. We now assume that the scale $x(t)$ at which production processes of date t are operated is exponentially increasing by the rate $g \geq 0$.

Total labour input at time t is then given by the sum of the labour inputs of all production processes at time t. Now the labour input at time t of a unit production process of date t' is given by α_T where $T=t-t'$. The scale of production processes of date t' is $x(t') = e^{gt'} x(0)$. So we have

$$L_t = \int_{-\infty}^{+\infty} e^{gt'} x(o) \alpha_{(t-t')} dt' = x(o) \int_{-\infty}^{+\infty} e^{-gT} e^{gt} \alpha_T dT$$

In a similar way we show that consumption C_t is given by

$$C_t = e^{gt} \, x(o) \int_{-\infty}^{+\infty} e^{-gT} \, c_T \, dT$$

Consumption per worker $c = \dfrac{C_t}{L_t}$ is therefore given by the equation

$$c \int_{-\infty}^{+\infty} e^{-gT} \alpha_T \, dT = \int_{-\infty}^{+\infty} e^{-gT} c_T \, dT$$

which shows that $c(g) = w(g)$. All the technological information relevant for the payoff between consumption per head and the steady state rate of growth is therefore contained in the wage interest curve. Moreover the two payoff functions are identical.

In a similar way as in part II we also can derive the derivative of T with respect to r. From the derivation there it follows that

$$\frac{dT_c}{dr} = -S_c^2(r) \qquad \frac{dT_\alpha}{dr} = -S_\alpha^2(r)$$

where S_c^2 is the variance of the distribution of outputs and $S_\alpha^2(r)$ is the variance of the distribution of inputs. Hence we get

$$\frac{dT}{dr} = S_\alpha^2 - S_c^2 \equiv +S$$

where we define S to be the difference between input variance and output variance. We then get for the second derivative of $w(r)$ that

$$\frac{d^2 w}{dr^2} = -T \frac{dw}{dr} - w \frac{dT}{dr} = w(T^2 - S)$$

For the logarithm of w we obtain

$$\frac{d\log w}{dr} = \frac{1}{w} \frac{dw}{dr} = -T(r)$$

$$\frac{d^2 \log w}{dr^2} = -\frac{dT}{dr} = -S(r)$$

It should be stated explicitly that S can be negative as well as positive. If S is negative, then the dispersion of outputs is greater than that of inputs. This case is not at all unrealistic. I am thinking of processes with comparatively high setup costs where the resources involved in the setup activity are labour intensive. What comes to one's mind are such activities as research and development, education and, to a lesser degree, construction of buildings for use in private consumption. These activities seem to increase their share in total national product. I am therefore not sure whether in reality S is positive or negative.

If S were zero then the point input - point output model would apply, at least as far as steady state properties are concerned. It would be an interesting question for empirical research to find out whether the standard production function model with a straight line as the wage interest curve for a given technique or the standard period of production model with a semi-log linear wage interest curve is the better simplifying paradigm for economic theory and empirical work.

It is perhaps worthwhile to mention that there is no good reason to exclude the technological possibility of a negative capital stock or a negative average period of production. The wage rate would then be an increasing function of the rate of interest. If the economy is organized along the lines of private ownership of means of production we may try to exclude this curiosum by assuming that a firm may be able to stop the process of production any time it wants. If this is so the capital value of a process of production never can become negative. It is also this assumption which allowed Arrow and Levhari to derive the uniqueness of the internal rate of return of processes of production. But this assumption is problematic. Firms may be obliged by law not to leave processes of production half finished, if this would cause negative external effects. But given that truncation is not allowed and given that the techniques available all have a negative period of production, it is unlikely to see the economy being organized with "private property of means of production". There will be too many difficulties to enforce payment of liabilities. Fortunately the world we live in happens to be such that we don't have to bother about this curiosum.

Chapter 2. The General Case of Joint Production and a General Nonsubstitution Theorem

We have so far assumed that it is possible to reduce the production processes to the two flows of primary inputs and final outputs. This is not possible in general, if joint production is allowed in the model. In this chapter we want to treat the more general case with joint production.

We take the discrete time model. The production possiblities are defined by a subset A of the nonnegative orthant of the 2n + 1 dimensional Euclidean space, where n is the number of different commodities. If and only if the vector $(L, y_1, \ldots y_n, x_1, \ldots x_n)$ is in A, can the economy produce the commodity vector $x = x_1, \ldots x_n$ by means of the produced inputs $y = y_1, \ldots y_n$ and the labour quantity L. The set A consists of all technically possible input - output combinations. The outputs become available one period after the inputs are available. But, as we did in the more special cases of discrete time models we assume that labour is paid at the end of the unit period.

The following conditions can be stated as equilibrium conditions. If x^*, y^*, L^* are equilibrium quantities, if p^*, are equilibrium prices and r and w are the interest rate and the wage rate respectively then the nonprofit condition implies

$$p_t^* x_t^* - (1+r_{t-1}) p_{t-1}^* y_{t-1}^* - w_t L_t^* = 0$$

$$p_t^* x - (1 + r_{t-1}) p_{t-1}^* y - w_t L \leq 0$$

for all (L, y, x) in A.

On the other hand, the demand for a commodity cannot exceed supply, and if supply exceeds demand the price must be zero. If z is the consumption vector we then have

$$p_t^* (x_t^* - y_t^* - z_t^*) = 0$$

$$p (x_t^* - y_t^* - z_t^*) \geq 0 \quad \text{for } p \geq 0$$

We shall not discuss the question of existence of an equilibrium here. What we shall discuss are the steady state specifications of the equilibrium conditions just introduced. For this purpose we again specify a standard commodity basket s in terms of which the real wage rate and real consumption per head are expressed. Without loss of generality we can limit our analysis to nonnegative price vectors which satisfy the equation ps = 1. We are then able to identify the nominal wage rate with the real wage rate, since we have $\bar{w}$ = wps and we can identify the nominal value of consumption with real consumption.

In a steady state (golden age) equilibrium prices are constant through time. The nonprofit condition then reads

$$p^* x_t^* - (1+r) p^* y_{t-1}^* - w L_t^* = 0$$

$$p^* (x - (1 + r) y) - w L \leq 0$$

for all (L, y, x) in A

In a steady state the quantities grow at the constant rate g. We therefore can write the demand supply conditions as

$$p^*(x_t^* - (1+g) y_{t-1}^* - z_t^*) = 0$$

$$p(x_t^* - (1+g) y_{t-1}^* - z_t^*) \geq 0$$

for all $p \geq 0$. If we restrict ourselves to price vectors with $p \geq 0$ and $ps = 1$ and if we define real consumption per head

$$c = \frac{p z_t^*}{L_t^*}$$

then the relations above can be written as

$$p^*(x_t^* - (1+g) y_{t-1}^*) - c L_t^* = 0$$

$$p(x_t^* - (1+g) y_{t-1}^*) - c L_t^* \geq 0$$

for all $p \geq 0$ with $ps = 1$

Now let the values with * refer to an equilibrium situation with some interest rate r and some growth rate g. Let the values with ^ refer to an equilibrium situation with the same interest rate r and a growth rate $\hat{g} = r$ and the same volume of labour used. The nonprofit condition and the supply-demand condition then imply

$$L_t w^* = p^*(x_t^* - (1+r) y_{t-1}^*) \geq p^*(\hat{x}_t - (1+r) \hat{y}_{t-1}) \geq$$

$$\geq \hat{p}(\hat{x}_t - (1+r) \hat{y}_{t-1}) = L_t \hat{w}$$

The first inequality follows from the nonprofit condition, the second inequality follows from the supply-demand condition when we keep in mind that $\hat{g} = r$. Thus we have shown: for a given interest rate the wage rate attains it's minimum when the rate of growth is equal to the rate of interest. This is if you wish the dual theorem of the golden rule of accumulation which we shall prove presently. We are no longer able to show that the wage interest curve is independent of the rate of growth of the system. The nonsubstitution theorem is not valid under such general conditions.

To prove the golden rule of accumulation in this model let the * variables be defined as above and let the ^ variables refer to a situation in which the same rate of growth rules as in the * situation but in which the rate of interest is equal to g. We then have

$$c^* L_t = p^* (x_t^* - (1+g) y_{t-1}^*) \leq$$

$$\leq \hat{p} (x_L^* - (1+g) y_{t-1}^*) \leq \hat{p} (\hat{x}_t - (1+g) \hat{y}_{t-1}) = \hat{c} L_t$$

The first inequality follows from the supply-demand condition the second inequality follows from the nonprofit condition. The combined inequalities prove that consumption per head for a given rate of growth is maximal if the rate of interest is equal to the rate of growth.

These two results can be used to derive a further inequality. In the more special case where the wage-interest curve was independent of the rate of growth we could derive the result that the wage interest curve **also** represented the payoff function between maximal consumption per head and the rate of growth. Now we have to say: maximal consumption per head for a given growth rate g is equal to the minimal wage for the given interest rate r=g. The minimum wage frontier is the maximum consumption frontier and this frontier separates the set of possible (w,r)-combinations from the set of possible (c,g)-combinations

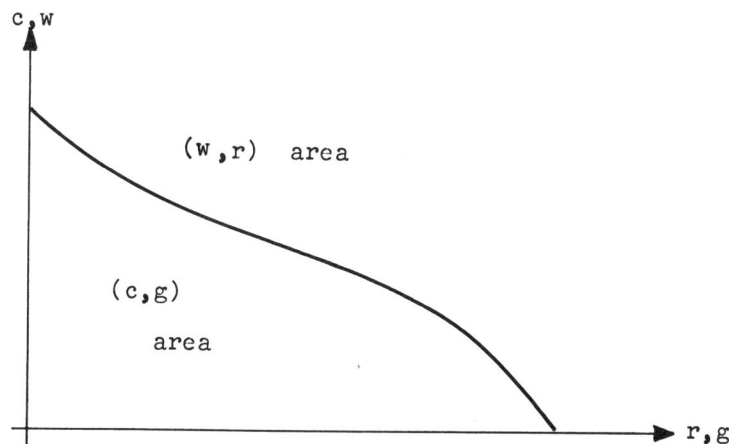

It is worthwhile to note that under the general conditions of joint production not only the nonsubstitution theorem but also any classical or Marxian or modern labour theory of value breaks down. It is no longer possible to define clearly what the specific labour content of a commodity or "the labour-time socially necessary for its production" is. This is borne out by the fact that even for a given rate of interest the price of a commodity depends on the rate of growth of the system.

In a global sense we can of course still determine the amount of labour contained in the sum of all consumption goods produced in a single period. If we give the labour inputs of time $t-\tau$ the weight $(1+g)^\tau$ then total labour inputs corrected with these weights are the same every period. The "value" of consumption good outputs remains the same even though the quantity increases exponentially. In terms of weighted labour inputs it is therefore clear that the quantity of labour contained in the consumption goods of period t is equal to the quantity of labour expended in period t.

We now want to show that the following three statements are equivalent. Each statement implies the other two statements. All three statements only apply to steady state situations.

1. For every nonnegative standard basket s the real wage-interest curve is independent of the quantities of commodities produced.

2. The specific labour content of a commodity can be defined for every interest rate and for every exponential weighting system of labour inputs and consumption good outputs and independently of the quantities of commodities produced.

3. For every interest rate the relative prices of commodities are determined independently of the quantities of commodities produced.

Let us assume that 1) is true. The real wage rate w for a given commodity basket is given by the equation $wps = \bar{w}$ where $\bar{w}$ is the nominal wage rate. Assume now that the vector s is given by $s = (1, 0, \ldots 0)$. Then the equation above reads $wp_1 = \bar{w}$ or $p_1 = \bar{w}/w$ or

$$\frac{p_1}{\bar{w}} = w$$

Since w is only a function of r the same is true for $\frac{p_1}{\bar{w}}$. In a similar way we find that $\frac{p_1}{\bar{w}}$ is only a function of r, or in general $\frac{p}{\bar{w}}$ is fixed whenever r is fixed. This implies statement 3).

The converse also holds. If 3) is true then clearly the real wage rate is determined for every s, whenever r is known.

3) implies 2). For any given interest rate r and any given γ consider a system growing at rate γ and using production techniques which have zero profit at interest rate r. Moreover the system sells to the consumption sector only some good i. By 3) the relative prices of all commodities are

given. By the supply demand equations the price of a commodity is zero, if there is excess supply. Thus by 3) there is no excess supply of any good whose relative price is not zero at this interest rate. We then are are able to impute all labour inputs to the final output i. Consider now a weighting system attaching weight $(1+\gamma)^{-t}$ to labour inputs of period t. Then, since unweighted labour inputs grow at rate γ, weighted labour inputs are constant. By the same argument weighted consumption good outputs are constant. The specific labour content of good i with weighting system $(1+\gamma)^{-t}$ with the technique applied can then be defined to be the coefficient of weighted labour inputs per period to weighted final outputs of good i. Hence we have given a natural definition of specific labour contents. Note that even for a given rate of interest r and a given weighting system γ the specific labour content need not be uniquely determined. If for instance r happens to be switch point of two techniques the specific labour content will depend on the technique mix which is applied. But for every mix of technique it is always possible to compute the real wage interest curve in terms of good i which is implied by the zero profit condition and by the physical outputs and inputs corresponding to a given technique mix and a given growth rate. This being so and keeping in mind the duality property of the wage interest curve for a given technique we actually can compute the labour input - final output ratio for a system growing at rate γ, by looking at the value of the wage rate of this wage interest curve at the interest rate γ. We therefore can actually compute the specific labour content of every good i for every weighting system $(1+\gamma)^{-t}$ from the national accounting data of a system, given that condition 3) is fulfilled. Note that this auxiliary wage interest curve can be computed from national accounting data because we keep the physical quantities and hence the techniques fixed. It is of course not identical with the wage interest curve of the economy which takes account of the possibilities of substitution.

2) implies 3). If 2) is valid apply for every given r the weighting system $(1+r)^{-t}$. Then the prices of commoditites must be equal to their specific labour contents and are thus independent of the composition of final demand, which proves 3).

It is perhaps a little pretentious to call this equivalence theorem a General Substitution Theorem. What it shows is the equivalence of the modern Non-Substitution condition and the possibility of defining specific labour contens. In view of this equivalence the modern search for nonsubstitution theorems can be seen as a continuation of the classical theory of price and value.

A careful examination of part II of these lecture notes shows that most results which were derived there carry over to the case of fixed capital as long as the wage interest curve of the economy is independent of the rate of growth and the composition of final output. By our equivalence theorem this is the case if and only if prices are independent of final demand and specific labour contents of commodities can be defined.

Part IV

General Equilibrium of Steady States

So far we have not introduced any consideration which would allow us to decide which point on the wage interest curve is being chosen by any given economy growing in a steady state. To solve this open problem we have to introduce the households in the economy and their intertemporal decisions. We first consider a single household whose lifetime extends from some periode t_o to some period $t_o+\lambda$. We assume perfect certainty and we assume that the wealth of the household is zero at t_o as well as at $t_o+\lambda$. We then have the following accounting identy

$$C_t + \dot{V}_t = W_t + rV_t$$

where C_t is consumption, W_t is earned income (wage income), V_t is wealth, r is the rate of interest and $\dot{V}_t$ is the rate of change of wealth, i.e. savings. This can be interpreted to be a differential equation for V_t. On integrating it we get

$$V_t = e^{r(t-t_o)}\left(V_{t_o} + \int_{t_o}^{t}(W_t - C_T)e^{-r(T-t_o)}dT\right)$$

Putting $t_o = 0$ and remembering that $V_{t_o} = 0$ and that $V_\lambda = 0$ we get the equation

$$0 = \int_0^\lambda (W_T - C_T)e^{-rT}dT$$

which is the equivalent to a budget constraint of the household for its decision with respect to the supply of labour and the demand for consumption goods.

We can now introduce a concept analogous to the concept of the average period of production. We call it the average waiting period. It is the mean time distance between the supply of labour and the demand of consumption goods by the household. It is

$$T = T_c - T_w$$

where T_c is the point of gravity of consumption good expenditure

$$T_c = \frac{\int_0^\lambda C_T e^{-rT} T\, dT}{\int_0^\lambda C_T e^{-rT}\, dT}$$

and T_w is the point of gravity of wage income

$$T_w = \frac{\int_0^\lambda W_T e^{-rT} T \, dT}{\int_0^\lambda W_T e^{-rT} T \, dT}$$

If we write $W_t = wM_t$ where w is the real wage rate then we can find the following result. Let there be a simultaneous change dr of the rate of interest and of the real wage rate dw. We ask the question whether the household is able to maintain the old $\{M_t, C\}$ path. For this we differentiate

$$\int_0^\lambda e^{-rT} C_T \, dT - w \int_0^\lambda e^{-rT} M_T \, dT$$

and we get

$$\left(-\int_0^\lambda T e^{-rT} C_T \, dT + w \int_0^\lambda T e^{-rT} M_T \, dT \right) dr$$

$$- \left(\int_0^\lambda e^{-rT} M_T \, dT \right) dw$$

We divide this expression by $\int_0^\lambda e^{-rT} C_T \, dT$ which equals $w \int_0^\lambda e^{-rT} M_T \, dT$

and get $\quad (-T_c + T_w) \, dr - \dfrac{dw}{w} = - T \, dr - \dfrac{1}{w} dw$

For positive dr this expression has the same sign as $- wT - \dfrac{dw}{dr}$. Thus whenever $- wT - \dfrac{dw}{dr} < 0$ then the change is such that the old path can be sustained since this means that the present value of consumption becomes smaller than the present value of wages. But this implies that utility rises, because now consumption can be raised keeping the labour supply the same. By a similar argument we see that utility falls if $- wT - \dfrac{dw}{dr} > 0$, and utility remains constant, if $\dfrac{dw}{dr} = - wT$. We get the the following table

$$\dfrac{dw}{dr} > - wT \quad \text{implies} \quad \dfrac{du}{dr} > 0$$

$$\dfrac{dw}{dr} = - wT \quad \text{implies} \quad \dfrac{du}{dr} = 0$$

$$\dfrac{dw}{dr} < - wT \quad \text{implies} \quad \dfrac{du}{dr} < 0$$

If we move along the wage interest curve as given by the technology then we have $\dfrac{1}{w} \dfrac{dw}{dr} = - T =$ - period of production. A rise in the rate of interest along the wage interest curve will improve the position of those households whose waiting period is greater than the period of production and it will hurt those who have a waiting period less than the period of production.

$$T > \bar{T} \text{ implies } \frac{du}{dr} > 0$$
$$T = \bar{T} \text{ implies } \frac{du}{dr} = 0$$
$$T < \bar{T} \text{ implies } \frac{du}{dr} < 0$$

In part II we have shown that a rise in the rate of interest will always have the effect of a substitution in the direction of reducing the period of production. Here we now can show that a rise in the rate of interest and a fall in the wage rate such that utility remains the same will tend to raise the average waiting period. Let r^o and w^o be given and let $\{C_T^o, w^o M_T^o\}$ be the corresponding consumption labour path. Let r^1, w^1 be another wage interest combination yielding the same utility as r^o, w^o. Let $\{C_T^1, w^1 M_T^1\}$ be the corresponding consumption labour path. We then have the inequalities

$$\int_0^\lambda (C_T^1 - w^o M_T^1) e^{-r^o T} dT \geq 0$$

$$\int_0^\lambda (C_T^o - w^1 M_T^o) e^{-r^1 T} dT \geq 0$$

Proof: If one of these inequalities would not hold it is easily seen by a revealed preference argument that not both paths would be utility maximizing. Indeed if for example

$$\int_0^\lambda (C_T^1 - w^o M_T^1) e^{-r^o T} dT < 0$$

then the budget constraint given by w^o, r^o would allow a path with more consumption than C_T^1 for every T, hence with more utility than $\{C_T^1, M_T^1\}$. Since $\{C_T^o, M_T^o\}$ is utility maximizing with respect to the same budget constraint this would imply that the utility of $\{C_T^1, M_T^1\}$ is smaller than the utility of $\{C_T^o, M_T^o\}$ which was excluded by assumption. In a similar way we obtain the other inequality.

Consider now the curve $w^*(r)$ defined by the equation

$$\int_0^\lambda (C_T^o - w^* M_T^o) e^{-rT} dT = 0$$

that is the set of all combinations (w^*, r) which are just sufficient for financing the path $\{C_T^o, M_T^o\}$. We then know that $w^1 \leq w^*(r^1)$.

In a similar way we define $w^{**}(r)$ by

$$\int_0^\lambda (C_T^1 - w^{**} M_T^1) e^{-rT} dT = 0$$

and we have $w^0 = w^*(r^0) \leq w^{**}(r^0)$. Also $w^1 = w^{**}(r^1)$. In a similar way as we have done above we can show that

$$\frac{dw^*}{dr} = - w^* T_0(r)$$

$$\frac{dw^{**}}{dr} = - w^{**} T_1(r)$$

where T_0 is the average waiting period of path $\{C_T^0, M_T^0\}$ evaluated at interest rate r and T_1 is the average waiting period of $\{C_T^1, M_T^1\}$

Assuming that $r_1 > r_0$ we therefore obtain the inequality

$$\int_{r_0}^{r_1} T_0(r) dr = - \int_{r_0}^{r_1} \frac{d\log w^*}{dr} dr = \log w^*(r_0) - \log w^*(r_1) =$$

$$= \log w^0 - \log w^*(r_1) \leq \log w^0 - \log w^1 \leq$$

$$\log w^{**}(r^0) - \log w^{**}(r_1) = - \int_{r_0}^{r_1} \frac{d\log w^{**}}{dr} dr =$$

$$= \int_{r_0}^{r_1} T_1(r) dr.$$ "On average" therefore the rise of the rate of interest causes a rise of the waiting period. In particular, if $r_1 - r_0$ is sufficiently small we get

$$\int_{r_0}^{r_1} T_0(r) dr \approx (r_1 - r_0) T_0(r_0) \leq \int_{r_0}^{r} T_1(r) dr \approx (r_1 - r_0) T_1(r_0)$$

Or, if r_1 is in a sufficiently small neighborhood of r_0

$$T_1(r_0) \geq T_0(r_0)$$

the waiting period is greater or equal, if evaluated at the same rate of interest. The following diagram illustrates what we just have shown.

We could draw indifference curves into the (w,r) diagram. A single indifference curve is the locus of all (w,r)-combinations yielding the same utility. The indifference curve is the inner envelope of all (w^*,r)-curves supporting $\{C_t, L_t\}$-paths with the given level of utility. By the envelope theorem the slope of the indifference curve at any given

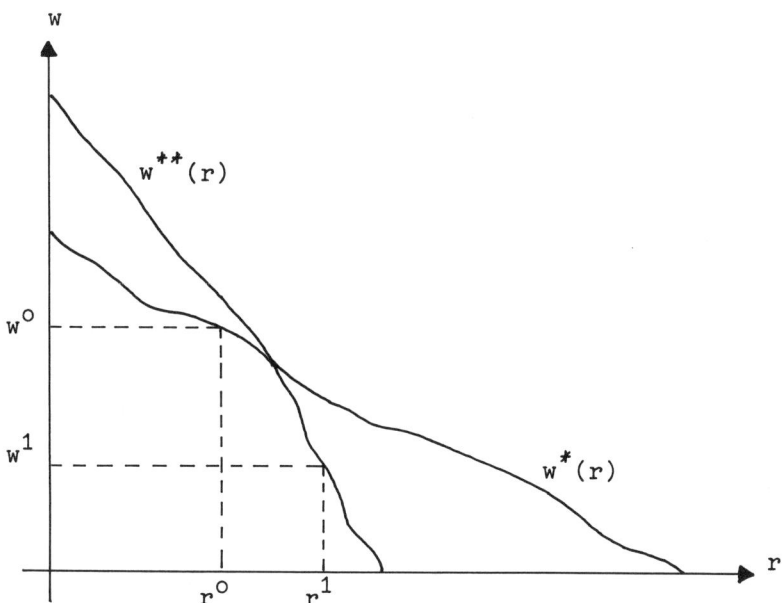

point is equal to the slope of the (w^*, r) curve going through this point which itself is equal to the average waiting period.

We shall now discuss the equilibrium in this economy. We start from the assumption that all households are alike in their preferences and that they all live for λ years. There is no inheritance of wealth in the economy. Population grows at the rate g, which means the number of households coming into existence at time t, N_t is exponentially growing: $N_t = N_o e^{gt}$. Total population at any given moment t is

$$N^t = \int_{t-\lambda}^{t} N_{t_o} \, dt_o = \frac{1-e^{-g\lambda}}{g} N_t$$

Total supply of labour time at moment t is given by

$$L_t = \int_{t-\lambda}^{t} N_{t_o} M_{t-t_o} \, dt_o = N_t \int_{t-\lambda}^{t} e^{-g(t-t_o)} M_{t-t_o} \, dt_o = N_t \int_{o}^{\lambda} e^{-g\tau} M_\tau \, d\tau$$

Total consumption $\bar{C}_t$ in the economy is given by

$$\bar{C}_t = \int_{t-\lambda}^{t} N_{t_o} C_{t-t_o} \, dt_o = N_t \int_{t-\lambda}^{t} e^{-g(t-t_o)} C_{t-t_o} \, dt_o = N_t \int_{o}^{\lambda} e^{-g\tau} C_\tau \, d\tau$$

Consumption per unit of labour supply is thus

$$c = \frac{\bar{c}_t}{L_t} = \frac{N_t \int_0^\lambda e^{-gT} C_T \, dT}{N_t \int_0^\lambda e^{-gT} M_T \, dT} = w^*(g)$$

where $w^*(r)$ is the wage rate necessary to support the given path $\{C_T, M_T\}$ at a rate of interest r. Hence - just as in the case of the production technology - a $w^*(r)$-curve derived from a given path $\{C_T, M_T\}$ has a dual interpretation as being the economy's consumption growth curve for the given individual consumption work pattern $\{C_T, M_T\}$.

Under conditions of equilibrium the supply of consumption goods per labour unit must be equal to the demand. Thus in equilibrium the wage interest curve of the technique used $w(r)$ and the wage interest curve of the consumption work pattern prevailing $w^*(r)$ must be equal at the prevailing interest rate and at the growth rate

$$w(r) = w^*(r) \text{ and } w(g) = w^*(g)$$

This is a necessary and sufficient condition for a steady state equilibrium if $r \neq g$. Apart from these two points r and g the two curves will in general be different. The time pattern of consumption and work of the households need of course not coincide with the pattern of labour inputs and consumption good outputs of the production technique. This is another application of the synchronization principle. While an isolated individual confronted with a single production opportunity of labour inputs and consumption goods outputs has no possibility to deviate in his work - consumption pattern from the technologically determined labour input consumption goods output flows this possibility exists if there are overlapping generations of households and production opportunities. This synchronization principle exerts its fullest force in golden age growth. Every deviation from the steady state has negative effects on the working of the synchronization principle. I believe that this principle is quite important for the welfare of most individuals and that this is among other things a reason why steady states will always be particularly important in the theoretical analysis of growth processes. In substance and form the synchronization principle has of course great similarities with the insurance principle under conditions of stochastically independent risks. And both are special cases of gains from trade.

It is easy to generalize our model by introducing several groups of households such that within each group households are homogeneous but between groups they are different. But we have to assume that each group grows at the same exponential rate g.

Before we proceed to prove the existence of an equilibrium we have to discuss what we mean by a market equilibrium if the rate of interest is equal to the rate of growth. If the rate of interest is equal to g then it follows that the demand for consumption goods per unit of labour offered is equal to the wage rate and this is independent of the specific time pattern of consumption and work. The wage rate is also equal to the production of consumption goods per head. Thus in a way the conditions of market equilibrium can be considered to be fulfilled for r =g no matter what the specific time patterns of the individual households and production processes are. Only by investigating in more detail what the institutional set up is can we decide whether such a constellation can be considered an equilibrium.

In the Arrow-Debreu theory of general equilibrium it is essentially assumed that all transactions of goods take place at the same moment of time. This assumption is clearly a difficult one for a model in which there exists no moment of time such that all relevant persons are alive. Let us for a moment assume that t and T are not time parameters, but, say, space parameters so that we are able to imagine complete simultaneity of all transactions. Then a "rate of interest" equal to g would in fact correspond to a possible general equilibrium: every firm maximizes profits, every household maximizes utility and all commodity and labour markets are cleared. It is essential that this spacial world is infinite: for every person and every individual process of production must be integrated in the same way, which, for $g \neq 0$, implies an infinite extension of the parameter t.

If t is again interpreted as time then complete simultaneity of transactions is impossible. Capital markets play the role of a substitute for transactions which cannot be performed now because at least one of the partners in the transaction does not exist. We can assume that there exists a market for bonds issued and bought by the different firms and households. In this way general claims on future conssumption goods can be bought and sold. Assume for example that the bonds have the form of perennial annunities (consols). Then each of them is a claim on a unit perennial flow of the consumption good. Because future transactions on the bond market are possible, bearers and issuers of these bonds are able to transform this infinte constant flow of consumption goods into any other flow of future consumption goods with the same present value. Thus, under conditions of certainty, and in a steady state, the form of claims on future consumption (e.g. consols) is not really relevant. It is not necessarily related to the substantive claims on future consumption goods and labour services which are determined by the techniques of production used and the set of consumption work pattern consistent with the budget constraints of the households. The possibility of recontracting on the bond market makes this severance of formal claims from actually anticipated deliveries possible, a severance which is necessary in a situation in which the future transactions of future generations are anticipated but cannot yet be performed.

So we replace all futures markets in labour and commodities by one market: the market in, say, consols. Now it turns out that at an interest rate $r = g$ the bond market is not necessarily in equilibrium. The supply of capital V_T of a household in its year T is given by the difference of the present value of future consumption and future wages. We thus get

$$V_T = \int_T^\lambda e^{-r(s-T)} (C_s - w M_s) \, ds$$

At time t there are $e^{-gT} N_t$ such households, whose supply of capital V_T^s then for $r = g$

$$V_T^s = e^{-gT} N_t \int_T^\lambda e^{-g(s-T)} (C_s - w M_s) \, ds = N_t \int_T^\lambda e^{-gs} (C_s - wM_s) \, ds$$

Total supply of capital is then

$$V^s = \int_0^\lambda V_T^s \, dT = N_t \int_0^\lambda \int_T^\lambda e^{-gs} (C_s - w M_w) \, ds \, dT =$$

$$= N_t \int_0^\lambda e^{-gs} (C_s - wM_s) \int_0^s 1 \, dT \, ds = N_t \int_0^\lambda e^{-gs} (C_s - wM_s) \, s \, ds$$

For the supply of capital per unit of the consumption good demanded we obtain (since $\bar{C}_t = wL_t$)

$$\frac{V^s}{\bar{C}} = \frac{N_t \int_0^\lambda e^{-gs} C_s \, s \, ds}{N_t \int_0^\lambda e^{-gs} C_s \, ds} - \frac{N_t \int_0^\lambda e^{-gs} wM_s \, s \, ds}{N_t \int_0^\lambda e^{-gs} wM_s \, ds}$$

$$= T_C - T_W = T$$

In a different way we have shown earlier that for $r = g$ demand for capital is $V^D = T \bar{C}$. Thus supply and demand on the capital market only coincide at $r = g$ if the average waiting period is equal to the average period of production. We thus consider the position $r = g$ only as an equilibrium, if $T(g) = \mathcal{T}(g)$. For $r \neq g$ equilibrium on the commodity markets implies equilibrium on the capital market.

It is not self evident that a steady state equilibrium exists. Indeed we easily can construct examples which do not have a steady state equilibrium. We shall give one below after having shown the following property of steady state equilibria: <u>In a steady state equilibrium there exists ρ lying between g and r such that for the weighting system $e^{-\rho t}$ the average period of production and the average waiting period of the households are equal.</u>

Proof: For the following let the parameter θ indicate the technique which is used in equilibrium. If several techniques are used simultaneously we can think of θ representing a mix of techniques. Since we will not vary θ we do not have to bother about mathematical properties of θ and of the dependence of w on θ. Let η stand for the consumption-work pattern which is used in equilibrium. The proposition is certainly true, if in equilibrium $r = g$, for then $T(g) = \mathcal{T}(g)$. If $r \neq g$ then we have the equation for $\theta = r$ $w(r,\theta) = w^*(r,\eta)$; $w(g,\theta) = w^*(g,\eta)$

$$w(\rho,\theta) T(\rho,\theta) = -\frac{\partial w(\rho,\theta)}{\partial \rho} \quad w^*(\rho,\eta) \mathcal{T}(\rho,\eta) = -\frac{\partial w^*(\rho,\eta)}{\partial \rho}$$

hence $\log w(r,\theta) = - \int_g^r T(\rho,\theta) d\rho + \log w(g,\theta)$

$\log w^*(r,\eta) = 1 - \int_g^r \mathcal{T}(\rho,\eta) d\rho + \log w^*(g,\eta)$

T and $\mathcal{T}$ are continuous functions of ρ. Thus by the mean value theorem there exists ρ^* such that

$$0 = \int_g^r (T(\rho,\theta) - \mathcal{T}(\rho,\eta)) d\rho = (r-g)(T(\rho^*,\theta) - \mathcal{T}(\rho^*,\eta))$$

ρ^* is the value of ρ which we were looking for.

In other words: if we take the average over all weighting systems $e^{-\rho t}$ for all ρ between g and r then the "average" average period of production and the "average" average waiting period are the same. In this weak sense it is true that equilibrium requires the waiting of consumers for consumption goods and to be in line with the waiting of producers for final outputs. This result suggests how we can easily find examples for which no steady state equilibrium exists. We have to find a technology which does not allow a period of production T less than λ, the lifetime of a household and combine this with the assumption that consumers do not leave wealth to their heirs. Take for example the point input point output model and assume that there is only the choice between techniques with T > λ. Now for any weighting system τ is less than λ. Hence there exists no ρ such that T (ρ) = τ (ρ). Therefore no equilibrium exists. No matter how high the rate of interest is, there will always be positive excess demand on the capital market.

This example already suggests which case causes a difficulty in proving existence of an equilibrium: The case in which excess demand for capital has the same sign for every rate of interest. It would be cumbersome and not terribly interesting to try to find various sufficient conditions to exclude such a case. It appears not to be very realistic.

In the following we will give an existence proof for a steady state equilibrium.

Theorem: A steady state equilibrium exists if (i) the number of different techniques available to the economy is finite, and every technique has a wage interest curve independent if the rate of growth (ii) the demand for consumption goods and the supply of labour of the household sector are continuous functions of the rate of interest and the wage rate, (iii) there exist two steady state constellations such that not both show the same sign for the excess demand for capital.

Condition (iii) is, as just shown above, essential and not trivially fulfilled. Conditions (i) and (ii) can be generalized if we are prpared to use more sophisticated mathematical techniques than the ones used in the present proof. Condition (ii) is fulfilled if preferences of consumers have the property of strict convexity of "the preferred sets". Modern general equilibrium theory shows that weak convexity would do as well and that nonconvexity can be dealt with if the economy is "large"

Proof of the theorem: Let $\theta = 1, 2, \ldots n$ be the parameter for the techniques available to the economy. Given the different wage interest curves $w(r,\theta)$ of the techniques the wage interest curve of the economy $w(r) = \max_{\theta} w(r,\theta)$ can be constructed. Since all $w(r,\theta)$ are continuous functions of r, the same is true for $w(r)$, the maximum of continuous functions is continuous. Let η be a parameter characterizing the different steady state consumption work patterns. Every consumption work pattern is characterized by a wage interest function $w^*(r,\eta)$ which gives the wage rate necessary to support pattern η for any given interest rate r. Choose the parameter η in such a way that it indicates the rate of interest at which this pattern is valid. Thus if $\eta = \bar{r}$, then η is the parameter value of the pattern prevailing at the rate of interest $\bar{r}$ and the wage rate $(w(\bar{r}) = \max_\theta w(\bar{r},\theta)$. By assumption (ii) and by the continuity of $w(r)$ the consumption work pattern varies continuously with r and hence with η.

Note that demand for capital per worker v^D is not necessarily uniquely determined for a given interest rate, if at this interest rate there are at least two techniques which maximize the wage rate. If only one technique is used demand for capital is equal to

$$v^D(r,\theta) = \frac{w(g,\theta) - w(r,\theta)}{r-g}, \quad r \neq g$$

$$v^D(g,\theta) = T(g,\theta)w(g,\theta) = -\frac{\partial w(r,\theta)}{\partial r}\bigg|_{r=g} =$$

$$= \lim_{r \to g} \frac{w(g,\theta) - w(r,\theta)}{r - g} = \lim_{r \to g} v^D(r,\theta)$$

If several θ can be applied at a given r, there is a whole interval of possible demands for capital, since the different technique can be used in any convex combination. To formalize this let $R(\theta)$ be defined by

$$R(\theta) = \{r \mid w(r,\theta) = w(r)\}$$

It is the range of interest rates at which technique θ is efficient. We then can define $\hat{\theta}(r)$ to be the set

$$\hat{\theta}(r) = \{\theta \mid r \in R(\theta)\}$$

i.e. the set of techniques which are efficient at r. Now demand for capital at the rate of interest r can be any number v^D which can be written as a convex combination of the $v^D(r,\theta)$. The set of admissible demands for capital $V^D(r)$ is given by

$$V^D(r) = \{v \mid v^D = \sum_{\theta \in \hat{\theta}(r)} \mu_\theta v^D(r,\theta) \text{ with } \sum_{\theta \in \hat{\theta}(r)} \mu_\theta = 1, \mu_\theta \geq 0\}$$

The supply of capital is given by

$$v^S(\eta) = \frac{w^*(g,\eta) - w^*(\eta,\eta)}{\eta - g}$$

Excess demand for capital is then
$$z = v^D - v^S(r)$$
Equilibrium exists whenever there exists $v^D \varepsilon V^D(r)$ such $v^D = v^S(r)$. We say the set $V^D(r) - v^S(r) > 0$ if for any $v^D \varepsilon V^D(r)$ we have $v^D - v^S(r) > 0$; similarly for $V^D(r) - v^S(r) < 0$. Now we show that the set $R^+ = \{ r : V^D(r) - v^S(r) > 0 \}$ and the set $R^- = \{ r: V^D(r) - v^S(r) < 0 \}$ are both open. To prove that R^+ is open assume that R^+ is not empty (otherwise R^+ is open because the empty set is open). Let $\bar{r} \varepsilon R^+$. Then $w(\bar{r}) = w(\bar{r}, \theta_1) = w(\bar{r}, \theta_2)$ for any $\theta_1, \theta_2 \varepsilon \hat{\theta}(\bar{r})$ and $w(\bar{r}, \theta) < w(\bar{r})$ for any $\theta \notin \hat{\theta}(\bar{r})$. Since the set of different θ is finite and since $w(r, \theta)$ is continuous in r we can find a neighborhood $N(\bar{r})$ such that $w(r, \theta) < w(r)$ for $\theta \notin \hat{\theta}(\bar{r})$ for $r \varepsilon N(\bar{r})$ which implies $\hat{\theta}(r) = \hat{\theta}(\bar{r})$ for $r \varepsilon N(\bar{r})$. Thus for $r \varepsilon N(\bar{r})$ we have

$$\min V^D(r) = \min_{\theta \varepsilon \hat{\theta}(\bar{r})} v^D(r, \theta). \text{ But}$$

$$v^D(r, \theta) = \frac{w(g, \theta) - w(r, \theta)}{r - g}$$ is a continuous function of r. It is also continuous at $r = g$ since, as we have shown $v^D(g, \theta) = \lim_{r \to g} v^D(r, \theta)$. Hence $\min_{\theta \varepsilon \hat{\theta}(\bar{r})} v^D(r, \theta)$ is continuous, hence $\min V^D(r)$ is continuous in $N(\bar{r})$. Hence there exists a neighborhood of $\bar{r}$, $N^o(\bar{r}) \varepsilon N(\bar{r})$ such that for $r \varepsilon N^o(\bar{r})$
or $V^D(r) - v^S(r) > 0$ or $V^D(r) - v^S(r) > 0$. Thus there exists a neighborhood $N^o(\bar{r})$ such that $r \varepsilon R^+$, if $r \varepsilon N^o(\bar{r})$. This proves that R^+ is open. In a similar way we show that R^- is open.

If R^+ and R^- were both empty every rate of interest would be consistent with an equilibrium. If R^+ is empty and R^- is not empty then by assumption (iii) there exists r such that excess demand is nonnegative. If it is zero at this r an equilibrium exists. If it is positive R^+ is not empty. Similarly, if R^+ is not empty then there either exists an equilibrium or R^- is not empty. Thus there only remains the case that both R^- and R^+ are not empty. But since both are open and since $R^- \cap R^+$ is empty the set $R^+ \cup R^-$ is not connected. But the real line R is connected, hence $R^+ \cup R^- \neq R$. There exists r which is neither contained in R^+ nor in R^-. This proves the existence of an equilibrium.

It should be noted that an equilibrium at $r = g$ can always be established, if there is an institution, say the government, which keeps bonds in its portfolio if there is excess supply of bonds or sells bonds, if there is excess demand for them, so that the capital market can come into equilibrium. The goods and labour markets clear automatically at $r=g$, if the government does not interfere in these markets. This implies that the net holdings of bonds by the government grow at the rate of interest which is equal to the rate of growth so that the system remains in steady state equilibrium. This is only so at $r=g$. Whenever the rate of interest is different from g either government net holdings grow at a different rate than other assets, i.e. we are not in a steady state equilibrium, or the government has to engage in net tradings on the commodity markets and thereby interfere in the market equilibrium.

This observation could serve as a starting point for a generalization of a theory of exploitation as we sketched it following Marx, in chapter 3 of part II. There we assume that of the two classes "workers" and "capitalists" only the latter class saves. The Marxian degree of exploitation in a model with technical progress and no population growth was equal to the amount of labour time devoted to the production of consumption goods for capitalists **divided** by the amount of time devoted to the production of consumption goods for the workers. As is well known many people are workers and at the same time owners of capital. This makes it more difficult to formulate a degree of exploitation of one class of people by another class of people.

Government interference in the accumulation process will affect different groups of people in a different way. If government policy shifts the steady state equilibrium from a higher to a lower interest rate - along the technologically given wage-interest frontier - one group of people will obtain a higher utility level other people will attain a lower utility level. This difference could be used as a criterion for an economic class distinction: we call "capitalists" those people whose utility rises (falls) as we move across steady states along the wage-interest frontier in the direction of a higher (lower) rate of interest. We call "workers" those people whose utility is inversely related to the prevailing steady state rate of interest. These definitions, unfortunately, are not precise except locally: there may be people whose utility is not a monotonic function of the steady state rate of interest. But Marxist theory (less so western economic theory) would consider it a methodical error to refrain from the use of the class concept simply because the question what the empirical criterion of class distinction is cannot unambiguously be answered. Moreover there may exist a solution to this problem in the properties of the golden rule path.

A steady state equilibrium usually implies that the different groups of people characterized by their different work consumption patterns keep their relative weight in the population and the economy. Each of these groups therefore grows at the same rate g. Given that this is so, it is easy to see that on the Golden Rule path each group only works for the production of its own consumption goods. The argument to show this is simple: clearly total population works only for the production of consumption goods for its own use. Now consider an economy in which only one of the different groups is present and in which, by means of a corresponding public debt policy of the government, the Golden Rule state prevails. Then in terms of production this economy is a mirror image of the original many group economy only at a smaller scale. The group which is present in this smaller economy firstly produces and consumer all consumption goods and is therefore not exploited by any other group and secondly is in terms of their consumption work pattern exactly in the same situation as it is in the larger economy. This shows that also in the larger many group economy any single group is not exploited by any other group.

Two things have to be made clear. The first is that a similar analysis is not possible for a steady state with $r \neq g$. For then, as was pointed out, the steady state equilibrium does explicitly depend on the aggregate savings behaviour of the population. The rate of interest and hence the work consumption pattern will be different in the single group economy and in the mixed group economy. Also, if the government has non-zero net holdings (positive of negative) of assets, it interferes on the commodity markets. The second thing to be remembered is the assumption that there is only one type of labour. As soon as we introduce different types of labour which are not complete substitutes of each other the separation of one group from the rest of the economy affects the production possibilities of this group. I think that a complete theory of exploitation will have to say something about the social and economic relations of different kinds of labour (e.g. male and female labour). But I do not want to discuss this interesting, important and complicated field of analysis here.

Whenever we distinguish more than two different groups the definition of exploitation becomes difficult, in particular if we want to quantify the rate of exploitation. We would have a whole matrix of rates of exploitation, but it seems to be impossible to define them in unambiguous way. The analogy of multilateral international trade will make this clear: if there are two countries and their balance of trade and services is not in equilibrium (assuming for simplicity that their net credit position does not change) then we can in some way consider one country's welfare being improved at the expence of the other. In multilateral trade it makes no sense to consider bilaterally balanced trade balances to be of significance. Only the overall balance of trade of every country is of interest. Similarly it makes no sense to define bilateral rates of exploitation between two groups, if more than two groups can be distinguished. We only can speak of rates of exploitation of a group in their relation with the total rest of the economy. In the spirit of Marx we define these rates of exploitation of any group as follows. Let L_{it} be the quantity of labour supplied by group i, let L^*_{it} be the quantity of labour expended at time t and used for the direct and indirect production of consumption goods to be consumed by group i. Then the rate of exploitation of group i is defined to be

$$R_i = \frac{L_{it} - L^*_{it}}{L^*_{it}} = \frac{L_{it}}{L^*_{it}} - 1$$

The rate of exploitation is positive if the group is exploited by the rest of the economy. The rate of exploitation is negative, if the group exploits the rest of the economy. If we concentrate on steady states we can write the rates of exploitation as functions of the steady state rate of interest $R_i = R_i(r)$. We then know already that $R_i(g) = 0$ for all i.

Of particular interest is of course the exploitation relation between "workers" and "capitalists". In the simple world in which capitalists don't work and workers don't accumulate our definition is basically the Marxian definition of exploitation. This is literally true when there is no population growth. In the more complicated case in which there is a large group of people who supply labour and accumulate capital we proposed to distinguish between capitalists and workers according to the criterion whether there exists an isotone or an antitone relation between the level of utility and the rate of interest. This definition can of course be given a less subjectivistic slant by the following reasoning: If the rate of interest rises and the wage rate falls accordingly there is one group of people who are able to maintain their former work consumption pattern and indeed are able to consume more in every period or work less in every period. They clearly benefit from the rise in the rate of interest and thus can be called capitalists. There is another group of people who are not able to maintain their former work consumtpion pattern due to the fact that the real wage rate has fallen. They can be called workers. We do not need the "bourgeois" concept of utility and preferences to introduce this definition of the two classes.

Another way to distinguish between these two classes is by using our definition of exploitation. Divide the population into groups which are internally homogeneous concerning work consumption patterns. For any given rate of interest $r > g$ count as "workers" those groups whose rate of exploitation $R_i(r)$ is positive and count as "capitalists" those groups whose $R_i(r)$ is negative. The rate of exploitation of workers by capitalists, $R(r)$, would then be given by

$$R = \frac{L_W}{L_W^*} - 1 = \frac{\sum_{i \in W} L_i}{\sum_{i \in W} L_i^*} - 1 =$$

$$= \frac{\sum_{i \in W} (R_i+1) L_i^*}{\sum_{i \in W} L_i^*} - 1 = \frac{\sum_{i \in W} L_i^* R_i}{\sum_{i \in W} L_i^*}$$

where the set of indices $w(r) = \{ i \mid R_i(r) > 0 \}$. The rate of exploitation of the working class is thus a weighted average of the rates of expolitation of those groups who are exploited. The weights are given by - in Marxian terms - the necessary labour time to reproduce the different groups, that is by the quantities of labour allocated to the production of consumption goods of these groups.

Both definitions of the class distinction depend on the rate of interest. There may exist groups which may belong to the capitalists at one rate of interest and to the workers at a different rate of interest. It is possible to relate both definitions to the capital theoretic concepts which we have used earlier. The first definition refers to the average waiting period if we use the weighting system e^{-rt}. As was shown earlier, a rise in the rate of interest improves the standard of living for those whose average waiting period is longer than the average period of production. Hence in this definition capitalists are those groups whose average waiting period is longer than the average period of production using the prevailing rate of interest, i.e. the prevailing price system as the weighting system. This definition corresponds to the traditional period of production approach to capital theory.

The other definition of class and exploitation can be related to the "supply and demand of capital" approach to capital theory. For a rate of interest $r \neq g$ the value of capital per worker is given by

$$v = \frac{c - w}{r - g} = \frac{w(g,\theta) - w(r,\theta)}{r - g}$$

where θ is the parameter of the technique (or mix of techniques) in actual use. Now a group which neither exploits nor is exploited has, as was shown earlier, a consumption per unit of labour expended which is equal to $w(g,\theta)$. For any group the budget constraint can be written

$$v_i = \frac{c_i - w(r,\theta)}{r - g}$$

where v_i is the amount of wealth (or capital supplied) and c_i the amount of consumption per unit of labour supplied. Hence for a group which is neither exploited nor exploiting we must have $v_i = v$. If a group belongs to the exploting class then clearly $c_i > w(g,\theta)$ and this implies for $r > g$

$$v_i > v$$

Similarly for the exploited groups we have

$$v_i < v$$

This justifies the name capitalists for the exploiting class and workers for the exploited. The latter are short of means of production (given the technique of production θ) and therefore have to work part of their time for the benefit of those groups which can supply the lacking means of production.

We have not yet made use of the consumption maximizing property of the Golden Rule path. If we are on a steady path with $r \neq g$ the loss in terms of consumption per labour unit for the exploited is twofold. Not only do they receive less than the full product of their work, but in addition less consumption goods per unit of labour are produced. Also some of those groups which we have considered exploiters may in fact receive a smaller amount of consumption goods. We could incorporate this loss in total production in a revised concept of exploitation, but this may lead to confusion. Similar attempts of Marx and modern Marxists like Baran and Sweezy to consider certain costs to the economy as part of surplus value or (in the case of Baran and Sweezy) of surplus are, I believe, confusing rather than helpful, indeed, I think, they are not consistent with an important concept of Marx, the "social character of production". There is no space here to argue this point in detail.

While we discuss the economic consequences of a deviation from the Golden Rule path we should state a theorem which is a pendant to the well known consumption maximizing property of the Golden Rule path. For a given household we can construct indifference curves in the wage interest diagram $w(r,u)$ combining different wage interest combinations of equal utility u. Let η be a parameter for the different consumption work patterns such that the parameter value η = r refers to the consumption work pattern prevailing in a situation where the rate of interest is r and the utility level obtained is $\bar{u}$. Let $w^*(r,\eta)$ be the wage rate necessary to support pattern η at the rate of interest r. For any given r the indifference curve representing utility level $\bar{u}$ will go through the point $w(r,\bar{u}) = w^*(r,r)$, that is the wage rate necessary to support the pattern η = r at the rate of interest r. On the other hand, as was already derived earlier, $w(r,\bar{u})$ is the lower envelope of the curves $w^*(r,\eta)$. Hence $w(r,\bar{u}) = w^*(r,r) = \min_\eta w^*(r,\eta)$. In addition we know that consumption per unit of labour $c(g,\eta)$ at the rate of growth g and pattern η is given by

$$c(g,\eta) = w^*(g,\eta)$$

If we now try to minimize consumption per unit of labour for a given level of utility across consumption patterns we get the result

$\min c(g,\eta) = \min w^*(g,\eta) = w^*(g,g) = w(g,\bar{u})$. The theorem says in other words: If the rate of interest is equal to the rate of growth the households implement a work consumption pattern which minimizes the consumption per unit of labour necessary to support a given level of utility. In its formal structure the theorem is symmetric to the Golden Rule theorem and so is the method of proof.

The theorem has the following implication. In a nonexploitative economy with a homogenous population, consumption per labour unit for this homogeneous group of consumers is restricted to the technologically determined production of consumption goods per worker. Compare the utility level on the Golden Rule path with the level on any other steady state path: consumption per unit of labour necessary to maintain the utility of the Golden Rule path is higher, actual production of consumption goods is lower than on the Golden Rule path. This clearly implies that utility is maximized on the Golden Rule path. If the population is not homogeneous it is not necessarily true that utility is maximized on the Golden Rule path. But by a similar argument it is easy, to show that for every rate of interest there must exist some group whose utility is not as high as on the Golden Rule path.

References to the Literature

In this section I want to present what is basically the reading list of the course on capital theory given in the Winter-Semester 1970/71 at the University of Heidelberg.

General References

E.von Böhm-Bawerk, Positive Theorie des Kapitals (1st edition 1889), English translation: Positive Theory of Capital, 1891

I.Fisher, The Theory of Interest, New York 1930

K.Marx, Das Kapital, three volumes (1867, 1885, 1894), English translation: Capital, Chicago 1906, 1909

F.A.Lutz, Zinstheorie, 2nd edition, Tübingen-Zürich 1967, English translation: The Theory of Interest, Chicago 1968

R.Dorfman, P.Samuelson, R.Solow (Dosso), Linear Programming and Economic Analysis, New York, Toronto, London 1958

P.Sraffa, The Production of Commodities by Means of Commodities, Cambridge, England, 1960

E.Burmeister, R.Dobell, Mathematical Theories of Economic Growth, New York 1970

J.Robinson, The Accumulation of Capital, London 1956

Preface. Classic sources of the concepts mentioned in the preface are: Marx,op.cit., volume I; Böhm-Bawerk, op.cit.; J.B.Clark, The Distribution of Wealth, New York 1899, chapter XX; A.Marshall, Principles of economics, London 1890. For Solow's work on the private and social rate of return see: R.M.Solow, Capital Theory and the Rate of Return, Amsterdam 1963. One of the most recent controversies is between Pasinetti and Solow in the Economic Journal (L.L.Pasinetti, Switches of Technique and the Rate of Return in Capital Theory, E.J. September 1969, R.M.Solow, On the Rate of Return: Reply to Pasinetti, E.J., June 1970, and L.L. Pasinetti, Again on Capital Theory and Solow's "Rate of Return", E.J. June 1970). I should also like to refer the reader to a controversy between Riese and myself in Kyklos, where I emphasize that the equality of social and private rate of return on investment is just a special case of the equality of price ratios and marginal rates of transformation in general equilibrium models (H.Riese, Das Ende einer Wachstumstheorie, Kyklos 1970, Fasc.4; C.C.von Weizsäcker, Ende einer Wachstumstheorie?, Kyklos 1971, Fasc.1; H.Riese, Das Finale vom Ende einer Wachstumstheorie, Kyklos 1971, Fasc.1). Hicks' theory is in J.R.Hicks, A Neo Austrian Growth Theory, Economic Journal, June 1970.

Part I, Capital Theory Without Capital

For a comprehensive treatment of general equilibrium theory see the forthcoming book of K.J.Arrow and F.Hahn, The Theory of General Equilibrium.

Chapter 1

Dosso, Chapter 9 and 10

W.Leontief, The Structure of the American Economy, 1919-1939, 2nd edition, 1951

P.Sraffa, Part I

Chapter 2

Dosso, Chapter 9 and 10

Burmeister-Dobell, Chapter 8

P.A.Samuelson, Abstract of a Theorem Concerning Substitutability in Open Leontief Models, in T.C.Koopmans (ed.) Activity Analysis of Production and Allocation, New York 1951

R.Shepard, Cost Functions and Production Functions, Princeton 1951

Chapter 3

Dosso, Chapter 9 and 10

P.A.Samuelson, Prices of Factors and Goods in General Equilibrium, in Collected Ec.Papers, Cambridge/Mass.-London, 1966, Vol.2, No.70

Part II, Circulating Capital

Chapter 1

R.M.Solow, A Contribution to the Theory of Economic Growth, Quart.J. of Ec., Vol.70, 1956, pp.65-94

P.A.Samuelson, Parable and Realism in Capital Theory: The Surrogate Production Function, Rev.Ec.Stud., Vol.29, 1962, pp.193-206

J.Robinson, The Production Function and the Theory of Capital, Rev.Ec.Stud., Vol.21, 1953/54, pp.81ff

R.M.Solow, The Production Function and the Theory of Capital, RES, Vol.23, 1955/56, pp. 101ff

J.Robinson, The Production Function and the Theory of Capital. A Reply, RES, Vol.23, 1955/56, pp.247ff

R.M.Solow, Growth Theory, An Exposition, Oxford 1970

Burmeister-Dobell, Chapter 2

Chapter 2

F.Engels, Anti-Dühring, Marx-Engels Werke, Vol.20, pp.288ff

Sraffa, Part I

E.v.Böhm-Bawerk, Zum Abschluß des Marxschen Systems, in: Festgabe für K.Knies, Berlin 1896, repr. in: Kleinere Abhandlungen über Kapital und Zins, Vol.II, Wien-Leipzig 1926, pp.321-435

M.Bruno, Fundamental Duality Relations in the Pure Theory of Capital and Growth, RES, Vol.36, 1969, pp. 39-55

C.C.von Weizsäcker, Bemerkungen zu einem Symposium über Wachstumstheorie und Produktionsfunktionen, Kyklos, Vol.16, 1963, pp. 438-455

Burmeister-Dobell, Chapter 7 and 8

M.Bruno, Optimal Patterns of Trade and Development, RESt., Vol.49, 1967, pp. 545ff

Chapter 3

K.Marx, Capital

Sraffa, Part I

P.A.Samuelson, Survey of the Marxian Transformation Problem, to be published in the Journal of Economic Literature, 1971

C.C.von Weizsäcker and P.A.Samuelson, A New Labour Theory of Value for Rational Planning Through Use of the Bourgeois Profit Rate, to be published in the Proceedings of the National Academy of Sciences, 1971

C.C.von Weizsäcker, Bemerkungen

Chapter 4

Böhm-Bawerk, Positive Theory of Capital

C.Menger, Grundsätze der Volkswirtschaftslehre, 1st.edition, Wien 1871

F.A.Lutz, The Theory of Interest, Chapter 1

E.Helmstädter, Linearität und Zirkularität des volkswirtschaftlichen Kreislaufs, Weltwirtschaftl.Archiv, Vol.94, 1965

E.Wolfstetter, Die Kapitaltheorie bei E.v.Böhm-Bawerk, Manuskript, Heidelberg 1970

Clark, Distribution of Wealth

Chapter 5

Böhm-Bawerk, Positive Theory of Capital

Lutz, The Theory of Interest, Chapter 1 and 2

Wolfstetter, Kapitaltheorie bei Böhm-Bawerk

K.Wicksell, Über Wert, Kapital und Rente, Jena 1893

Chapter 6

Wicksell, Über Wert, Kapital und Rente

K.Wicksell, Vorlesungen über Nationalökonomie, Vol.I, Jena 1913

J.R.Hicks, Value and Capital, 1939

C.C.von Weizsäcker, Die zeitliche Struktur des Produktionsprozesses und das Problem der Einkommensverteilung zwischen Kapital und Arbeit, Weltwirtschaftl.Archiv, 1971

Chapter 7

P.A.Samuelson, Parable and Realism...
    Symposium "Paradoxes in Capital Theory", Quart.J.of Ec., Vol.80, 1966, pp.503-583 with the following articles: P.A.Samuelson, D.Levhari, The Nonswitching Theorem in False; P.Garegnani, Switching of Techniques; L.Pasinetti, Changes in the Rate of Profit and Switches of Techniques; M.Morishima, Refutation of the Nonswitching Theorem; M.Bruno, E.Burmeister, E.Sheshinski, The Nature and Implications of the Reswitching of Techniques, P.A.Samuelson, A Summing Up.

J.Robinson, K.A.Naqvi, The Badly Behaved Production Function, QJE, Vol.81, 1967, pp. 579ff

Sraffa, Part III

Burmeister-Dobell, Chapter 8

Chapter 8

P.A.Samuelson, A New Theorem on Non-Substitution, in: H.E.Hegland (ed.), Money, Growth and Methodology. Essays in Honor of J.Akerman Lund 1961, pp.407ff

J.A.Mirrlees, The Dynamic Non-Substitution Theorem, RES, Vol.36, 1969, pp.67ff

J.R.Hicks, Theory of Wages, London 1932, p.117 and p.245 (introduced the concept of elasticity of substitution)

Chapter 9

R.M.Solow, Capital Theory and the Rate of Return

J.E.Stiglitz, On Transitions between Steady States, Cowles Foundation, Discussion Paper No.306, January 1971

E.Phelps, The Golden Rule of Accumulation, Am.Ec.Rev., Vol.51, 1961, pp.638-643

C.C.von Weizsäcker, Wachstum, Zins und optimale Investitionsquote, Part II, Basel-Tübingen, 1962

Production Function Symposium 1962, with the articles in RES, Vol.29, 1962: J.Robinson, A Neo-Classical Theorem, pp.219ff; J.E.Meade, The Effect of Savings on Consumption in a State of Steady Growth, pp.227ff; Comments by J.Robinson (p.258), P.A.Samuelson (p.251) and Solow (p.255)

Burmeister-Dobell, Chapter 9

C.C.von Weizsäcker, Bemerkungen ...

M.Bruno, Fundamental Duality Relations ...

Part III, Fixed Capital

Chapter 1

Sraffa, Part III

R.M.Solow, A Contribution to the Theory of Economic Growth

K.J. Arrow, D.Levhari, Uniqueness of the Internal Rate of Return with Variable Life of Investment, E.J., Vol.79, 1969, pp.560-566

Chapter 2,

E.Burmeister, K.Kuga, The Factor-Price Frontier, Duality and Joint Production, RES, Vol.37, 1970, pp.11-19

J.Stiglitz, Non-Substitution Theorems with Durable Capital Goods, RES, Vol.37, 1970, pp.543-553

Part IV General Equilibrium of Steady States

J.E.Meade, Life-Cycle Savings, Inheritance and Economic Growth, RES, Vol.33, p.61-78

J. Tobin, Life-Cycle Saving and Balanced Growth, in Ten Economic Studies in the Tradition of Irving Fisher, New York-London-Sidney 1967, p.231-256

H.G.Nutzinger und E.Wolfstetter, Überlegungen zur Marxschen Ökonomie, Manuskript, Heidelberg 1970

Lecture Notes in Operations Research and Mathematical Systems

Vol. 1: H. Bühlmann, H. Loeffel, E. Nievergelt, Einführung in die Theorie und Praxis der Entscheidung bei Unsicherheit. 2. Auflage, IV, 125 Seiten 4°. 1969. DM 12,–

Vol. 2: U. N. Bhat, A Study of the Queueing Systems M/G/1 and GI/M/1. VIII, 78 pages. 4°. 1968. DM 8,80

Vol. 3: A. Strauss, An Introduction to Optimal Control Theory. VI, 153 pages. 4°. 1968. DM 14,–

Vol. 4: Einführung in die Methode Branch and Bound. Herausgegeben von F. Weinberg. VIII, 159 Seiten. 4°. 1968. DM 14,–

Vol. 5: L. Hyvärinen, Information Theory for Systems Engineers. VIII, 205 pages. 4°. 1968. DM 15,20

Vol. 6: H. P. Künzi, O. Müller, E. Nievergelt, Einführungskursus in die dynamische Programmierung. IV, 103 Seiten. 4°. 1968. DM 9,–

Vol. 7: W. Popp, Einführung in die Theorie der Lagerhaltung. VI, 173 Seiten. 4°. 1968. DM 14,80

Vol. 8: J. Teghem, J. Loris-Teghem, J. P. Lambotte, Modèles d'Attente M/G/1 et GI/M/1 à Arrivées et Services en Groupes. IV, 53 pages. 4°. 1969. DM 6,–

Vol. 9: E. Schultze, Einführung in die mathematischen Grundlagen der Informationstheorie. VI, 116 Seiten. 4°. 1969. DM 10,–

Vol. 10: D. Hochstädter, Stochastische Lagerhaltungsmodelle. VI, 269 Seiten. 4°. 1969. DM 18,–

Vol. 11/12: Mathematical Systems Theory and Economics. Edited by H. W. Kuhn and G. P. Szegö. VIII, IV, 486 pages. 4°. 1969. DM 34,–

Vol. 13: Heuristische Planungsmethoden. Herausgegeben von F. Weinberg und C. A. Zehnder. II, 93 Seiten. 4°. 1969. DM 8,–

Vol. 14: Computing Methods in Optimization Problems. Edited by A. V. Balakrishnan. V, 191 pages. 4°. 1969. DM 14,–

Vol. 15: Economic Models, Estimation and Risk Programming: Essays in Honor of Gerhard Tintner. Edited by K. A. Fox, G. V. L. Narasimham and J. K. Sengupta. VIII, 461 pages. 4°. 1969. DM 24,–

Vol. 16: H. P. Künzi und W. Oettli, Nichtlineare Optimierung: Neuere Verfahren, Bibliographie. IV, 180 Seiten. 4°. 1969. DM 12,–

Vol. 17: H. Bauer und K. Neumann, Berechnung optimaler Steuerungen, Maximumprinzip und dynamische Optimierung. VIII, 188 Seiten. 4°. 1969. DM 14,–

Vol. 18: M. Wolff, Optimale Instandhaltungspolitiken in einfachen Systemen. V, 143 Seiten. 4°. 1970. DM 12,–

Vol. 19: L. Hyvärinen, Mathematical Modeling for Industrial Processes. VI, 122 pages. 4°. 1970. DM 10,–

Vol. 20: G. Uebe, Optimale Fahrpläne. IX, 161 Seiten. 4°. 1970. DM 12,–

Vol. 21: Th. Liebling, Graphentheorie in Planungs- und Tourenproblemen am Beispiel des städtischen Straßendienstes. IX, 118 Seiten. 4°. 1970. DM 12,–

Vol. 22: W. Eichhorn, Theorie der homogenen Produktionsfunktion. VIII, 119 Seiten. 4°. 1970. DM 12,–

Vol. 23: A. Ghosal, Some Aspects of Queueing and Storage Systems. IV, 93 pages. 4°. 1970. DM 10,–

Vol. 24: Feichtinger, Lernprozesse in stochastischen Automaten. V, 66 Seiten. 4°. 1970. DM 6,–

Vol. 25: R. Henn und O. Opitz, Konsum- und Produktionstheorie I. II, 124 Seiten. 4°. 1970. DM 10,–

Vol. 26: D. Hochstädter und G. Uebe, Ökonometrische Methoden. XII, 250 Seiten. 4°. 1970. DM 18,–

Bitte wenden/Continued

Vol. 27: I. H. Mufti, Computational Methods in Optimal Control Problems.
IV, 45 pages. 4°. 1970. DM 6,–

Vol. 28: Theoretical Approaches to Non-Numerical Problem Solving. Edited by R. B. Banerji and M. D. Mesarovic. VI, 466 pages. 4°. 1970. DM 24,–

Vol. 29: S. E. Elmaghraby, Some Network Models in Management Science.
III, 177 pages. 4°. 1970. DM 16,–

Vol. 30: H. Noltemeier, Sensitivitätsanalyse bei diskreten linearen Optimierungsproblemen.
VI, 102 Seiten. 4°. 1970. DM 10,–

Vol. 31: M. Kühlmeyer, Die nichtzentrale t-Verteilung. II, 106 Seiten. 4°. 1970. DM 10,–

Vol. 32: F. Bartholomes und G. Hotz, Homomorphismen und Reduktionen linearer Sprachen.
XII, 143 Seiten. 4°. 1970. DM 14,–

Vol. 33: K. Hinderer, Foundations of Non-stationary Dynamic Programming with Discrete Time Parameter.
VI, 160 pages. 4°. 1970. DM 16,–

Vol. 34: H. Störmer, Semi-Markoff-Prozesse mit endlich vielen Zuständen. Theorie und Anwendungen.
VII, 128 Seiten. 4°. 1970. DM 12,–

Vol. 35: F. Ferschl, Markovketten. VI, 168 Seiten. 4°. 1970. DM 14,–

Vol. 36: M. P. J. Magill, On a General Economic Theory of Motion. VI, 95 pages. 4°. 1970. DM 10,–

Vol. 37: H. Müller-Merbach, On Round-Off Errors in Linear Programming.
VI, 48 pages. 4°. 1970. DM 10,–

Vol. 38: Statistische Methoden I, herausgegeben von E. Walter. VIII, 338 Seiten. 4°. 1970. DM 22,–

Vol. 39: Statistische Methoden II, herausgegeben von E. Walter. IV, 155 Seiten. 4°. 1970. DM 14,–

Vol. 40: H. Drygas, The Coordinate-Free Approach to Gauss-Markov Estimation.
VIII, 113 pages. 4°. 1970. DM 12,–

Vol. 41: U. Ueing, Zwei Lösungsmethoden für nichtkonvexe Programmierungsprobleme.
IV, 92 Seiten. 4°. 1971. DM 16,–

Vol. 42: A.V. Balakrishnan, Introduction to Optimization Theory in a Hilbert Space.
IV, 153 pages. 4°. 1971. DM 16,–

Vol. 43: J. A. Morales, Bayesian Full Information Structural Analysis. VI, 154 pages. 4°. 1971. DM 16,–

Vol. 44: G. Feichtinger, Stochastische Modelle demographischer Prozesse.
XIII, 404 pages. 4°. 1971. DM 28,–

Vol. 45: K. Wendler, Hauptaustauschschritte (Principal Pivoting). II, 64 pages. 4°. 1971. DM 16,–

Vol. 46: C. Boucher, Leçons sur la théorie des automates mathématiques.
VIII, 193 pages. 4°. 1971. DM 18,–

Vol. 47: H. A. Nour Eldin, Optimierung linearer Regelsysteme mit quadratischer Zielfunktion.
VIII, 163 pages. 4°. 1971. DM 16,–

Vol. 48: M. Constam, Fortran für Anfänger. VI, 143 pages. 4°. 1971. DM 16,–

Vol. 49: Ch. Schneeweiß, Regelungstechnische stochastische Optimierungsverfahren.
XI, 254 pages. 4°. 1971. DM 22,–

Vol. 50: Unternehmensforschung Heute – Übersichtsvorträge der Züricher Tagung von SVOR und DGU, September 1970. Herausgegeben von M. Beckmann. IV, 133 pages. 4°. 1971. DM 16,–

Vol. 51: Digitale Simulation. Herausgegeben von K. Bauknecht und W. Nef. IV, 207 pages. 4°. 1971. DM 18,–

Vol. 52: Invariant Imbedding. Proceedings of the Summer Workshop on Invariant Imbedding Held at the University of Southern California, June – August 1970. Edited by R. E. Bellman and E. D. Denman.
IV, 148 pages. 4°. 1971. DM 16,–

Vol. 53: J. Rosenmüller, Kooperative Spiele und Märkte. IV, 152 pages. 4°. 1971. DM 16,–

Vol. 54: C. C. von Weizsäcker, Steady State Capital Theory. III, 102 pages. 4°. 1971. DM 16,–